In memory of Dr. Abram Spiro, former Chairman of the Department of Near Eastern Languages and Literature, Wayne State University, Detroit, whose direction and friendship meant all the world to me.

I wish to give special thanks to my editors and researchers Ms. Ada Stern and Mr. Tom Downey from the period of the mid 1960's in relation to the original manuscript.

Order this book online at www.trafford.com
or email orders@trafford.com

Most Trafford titles are also available at major online book retailers.

Note for Librarians: A cataloguing record for this book is available from Library
and Archives Canada at www.collectionscanada.ca/amicus/index-e.html

Printed in the United States of America.

ISBN: 978-1-4251-0024-7 (sc)
ISBN: 978-1-4269-8789-2 (e)

Trafford rev. 02/29/2012

www.trafford.com

North America & international
toll-free: 1 888 232 4444 (USA & Canada)
phone: 250 383 6864 ◆ fax: 812 355 4082

CONTENTS

Introduction

The title of this book <u>Jesus Was Not a Christian</u> will startle thousands of Christians throughout the world. To devout Christians such an opinion of Jesus is contrary to the traditional portrayal by clergymen. To the Christians Jesus Christ was all that they think the Gospels say he was, the founder of Christianity, the God incarnate Messiah, conceived by the virgin Mary and dedicated to spreading the message of salvation to the Gentiles.

It is often difficult for Christians to accept that contrary though valid opinion exists about their faith, because from their childhood on they have been told that nothing can be questioned, that to deny Jesus Christ was to reject God and forfeit eternal salvation. Compounding this conditioning is the painful and threatening issue they must face: Can their parents, hundreds of devotional texts and organizations, the various Christian denominations, their friends who belong to them and the good ministers and priests be wrong? It takes an exceptional man or woman to face up to this. It takes the kind of person who cherishes the truth above all.

<u>Jesus Was Not A Christian</u> is the result of over 40 years of careful study of Christianity. Perhaps the most startling fact that I have uncovered from my study of the New Testament over the years is that this corpus of books is not describing one man when it refers to Jesus. The New Testament describes two different men called Jesus.

The first Jesus appeared at the beginning of the first century. There is not sure way of knowing when or where he was born because the records differ on these matters. It is known, however, that his Jew named Jesus considered himself to be a descendant of the house of King David, and that he and his twelve followers believed bravely, valiantly and with constancy that he was the God sent King of Jewish people, the Messiah, a title which when translated from the Greek means 'Christos' or Christ, roughly corresponding to the Hebrew 'Anointed One'. Jesus considered it his task to initiate the Kingdom of God on earth and reign over the Jews with righteousness and justice for the remainder of human time. This first Jesus was a man of deep faith and abiding conviction in the plan of God for messianic deliverance, though he never claimed to be more than a simple man created as the Bible has it 'in the image of God', or that his interpretation of the Messiahship differed from what was accepted by Jews at the time. In the truest sense, this Jesus was a King, for he had regal bearing and qualities of leadership; he had self-assurance and was a man of deep moral purpose. But all his qualities and convictions were wasted when he was judged by officials of the Roman Empire to be different and therefore dangerous and subsequently crucified as a criminal. This was the 'Jesus of History'.

The second Jesus never really lived. He is a composite and more often contradictory personality who is described in the New Testament as God the Son Incarnate. This is the Jesus who is credited with founding the Christian Church. He is the product of falsifications, misunderstandings, epileptic seizures of Paul of Tarsus and a natural inclination to search the Bible for hidden meanings. Historians have come to call this character the 'Jesus of Theology'.

Undoubtedly, most Churchmen are not prepared to admit that there is a difference between the Jesus of history and theology. A few will hint at a halfway admission that the Christian church under God's inspiration has come to be better informed about Jesus that he was about himself. What is not easily understood is the basic cause why Christian thinking demands the belief of God through the personality of Jesus. There is still a primitive fear of another Dimension beyond human comprehension. The Christian man, therefore, solicits peace of mind in the idea that this other dimension might be brought into association with himself in a way that pacifies his fear of what is alien. For the Christian, a genuine acknowledgement of God's approval of such a relationship is evidenced by what Churchmen teach about His act of temporary embracement of the human condition in the form of Jesus to save mankind. By separating the Jesus of history and theology the above mentioned relationship is destroyed. Accordingly, churchmen must steadfastly hold to the idea of the unity of the two Jesus in order to salvage their peace of mind as embodied in Christian logic.

Now that the reader has some understanding of what Christianity is and how difficult it is for those committed to this world religion to undertake an objective study of its origins and internal contradictions, I feel that it is incumbent upon me to describe how our study in this book will develop. The first section 'Jesus' is not a biography, but rather an attempt to uncover what Jesus actually taught and what he taught about himself and to develop a better understanding of concepts such as Messiah, Son of God and Lord which are used so frequently in the New Testament. An honest attempt has been made by the writer to get at and dissect the crucial issues concerning the death and resurrection of Jesus.

In section two 'The Rise of Christianity' I seek to tell the untold or often distorted story of how the work of Jesus was transformed into a universal religion. Concerning the rise of Christianity most Christians and Jews are absolutely ignorant: and for this reason I have spent much of the book on this subject in order to show that in the early Church martyrdom and sainthood were not of the slightest importance to its development. What did the closest associates of Jesus think about him? What effect did the Jewish War have on Christian origins? What is the true story involving the Gospels? What part did criminal forgery play in Christian history? These and many more questions will be answered with no holds barred.

For several years books have appeared that have offered preposterous theories about the origins, intentions and death of Jesus. I have not written one of these books. The theory that I offer is one that I feel is consistent with the New Testament. I present a book to you the reader with the assurance that for the first time a book about Jesus weighs what is said in the New Testament with what actually took place after the death of Jesus.

Arnim von Brachdte, D.D.

August 2, 2004

SECTION 1

JESUS

'Jesus was not a Christian, he was a Jew'
J. Wellhausen

1

The Coming of the Messiah

'Think not that I have come to destroy the Law, but to fulfill it.' Do not give to the dogs what is holy, neither cast your pearls before swine (Gentiles), or they will trample them under their feet and turn and tear you.' 'Do not go to the way of the Gentiles, or the Samaritan cities: go rather to the lost sheep of Israel.'

Jesus

The essential message of Jesus of Nazareth was that he was the Messiah. This was the faith on which the entire gospel rested, the faith expressed in the Synoptic Gospels, Mark, Matthew and Luke and the Fourth Gospel. John, of the New Testament book, with the dramatic recognition, 'You are the Messiah.'[1]

While Christians have proclaimed the Messiahship of Jesus, they have all along refused to consider the understanding that the Jews had attained about the Messiah and his mission, based on an intelligent reading of the scriptures. Consequently, numerous misconceptions have resulted about messianic prophecies and the preaching of Jesus. For instance, it is popular today in keeping with the spirit of ecumenism to forgive the Jewish people the murder of Jesus. Churchmen assert that the Jews were forced in good conscience to reject Jesus[2] because the Jewish Messiah was expected to be an advocate of violence and Jesus was a man of peace.[3]

What proof is there for this contention? Certainly it does not rest on any historical fact. The scripture had not endorsed violence, and men who advocated violence as a means for liberating the Jews from their oppressors were repudiated by the fraternity of the Pharisees who were the spiritual instructors of most Jews at the time.

Based on the prophecies of Isaiah and Jeremiah, the Psalms of Solomon described the type of Messiah who was anticipated by most Jews in the first century BC:

'...A righteous king and taught by God who reigns over them and there will be no iniquity in his days in their midst, for all will be holy and their king is... Messiah. He will not put his trust in horse and rider and bow, now will he acquire gold for war, not by ships will he gather confidence... Since he will strike the earth and the word of his mouth... he is pure from sin, so that he may rule a mighty nation, and chastise princes and overthrow sinners by the might of his word.'[4]

The Messiah was not a man of violence, but one of peace. His weapons, so to speak, were righteousness and justice. For over three hundred years before the coming of Jesus this description was considered authoritative by the majority of the Jewish people. This is the description of the Messiah with which churchmen should have familiarized themselves.

The Pharisees discussed these matters in the synagogues. While most Jews accepted their preachments as inspired by God, a few did not. Social outcasts, these isolated sectaries conceived the Messiah to be more than a national and political character: the Messiah was a pre-existent, heavenly man whose kingdom was more spiritual than political. In the book of Daniel this philosophy was set forth:

'As the visions during the night continued, I saw one as the Son of Man coming, on the clouds of heaven; when he reached the Ancient One and was presented before him, he received dominion, glory and kingship; nations and peoples of every language submit to him.'[5]

Because the sectarians jealously guarded these apocalyptic dreams and visions, most Jews were not familiar with the Son of Man messianism. A man who claimed to be the Son of Man would not have enjoyed the support of the masses.

It is often said that the coming of the Messiah did not dominate the thinking of the Jewish people all the time. That is true. Contrary to popular Christian notions the Jews did not bite their fingernails for centuries in anticipation of the Messiah, and Jewish women did not sit on pins and needles waiting to be impregnated by the Holy Spirit. Everyday human problems as well as the relatively good circumstances under which the Jews lived when they were captives of certain pagan nations made sunrise to sundown contemplation of a Messiah virtually impossible. Interest in the coming of the Messiah, however, did intensify after 150 BC. And there was good reason for this.

Four circumstances may be chosen which contributed to the intensification of Messianic interest from the second century BC onward. First, poor political conditions had befallen the Jewish people when in 63 BC they were finally subjected by the Roman Empire. In Judea especially, where the cruel Roman-lackey King Herod the Great ruled, murders and harsh repression were commonplace. [6] Second, vast inequities existed in regard to Roman taxation. It was not progressive and had reached twenty-five percent by the first century. Third, the economic opportunities in Palestine were at the least unfavorable for the Jews. Fourth, perhaps as a result of the poor social, political and economic circumstances with which the Jews were forced to live after 150 BC, religious sects began to flourish. The Sadducees, the Pharisees and the Essenes were the most prominent. [7] They all in varying degrees attempted to instill in the people some appreciation of their religion, and, in the case of the Pharisees and Essenes, it was held that God had not forgotten his people.

All men were not effected the same way. Most were practical and contented themselves with a renewed hope in the Messiah's advent. For a minority, however, whose watch word was activism, the hurdles were convoluted. The Jewish Zealot party, for instance, mistakenly thought violence was the answer. Even the Samaritans responded, but the actions of their Messiah, the Taheb, resulted in only more violence. A few Jews, those men for whom the bounds of reality and fantasy were not well defined, even claimed to be Messiahs. [8] One such man, Jesus of Nazareth, would have been listed as one more contemporary failure if it had not been for the development of a religion that was wrongly named after him and that suffers from the delusion that he willed its existence. [9]

Study Aids

1. Matt. 15. 16-19

2. This view is not supported in the Gospels, and it is difficult to tell at what point in Church history it became popular.

3. See Joseph Klausner, <u>Messianic Idea in Israel</u>

4. <u>Psalms of Soloman</u>, 17.35-42

5. Dan, 7.13-14

6. <u>Josephus, Antiq.</u>, bk 15, Ch. 10.4; Assumption of Moses, 6.2-6

7. Grant, <u>Historical Introduction to the New Testament</u>, pp. 257-267

8. Harnack, A. Von. Die Mission und Ausbreitung des Christentums in den ersten drei Jahrhunderten, 2 Bande, Leipzig, 1906. Marcion: Das Evangelium vom Fremden Gott (Texte und Untersuchungen zure Geshichte der altchristlichen Literatur, herausgegeben von A. von Harnack und C. Schmidte, 3. Reihe 15 Band.) Leipzig, 1924.

9. Windish, H. Der Untergang Jerusalms (Anno 70) im Urtheil der Christen und Juden, article in Theologisch Tijdschrift, Leiden 1914. Der messianische Krieg und das Urchristentum, Tubigen, 1909.

2

Messiah Jesus

'The proclamation of Jesus must be viewed within the
framework of Judaism, Jesus was not a "Christian",
but a Jew, and his preaching is couched in the thought
forms and imagery of Judaism.'

Rudolph Bultmann

Strangely enough, while the Christian Church teaches the Jesus was
the incarnate Son of God who came to achieve spiritual salvation of the
Gentiles through his death on the cross, there is a substantial amount
of tradition in the Gospels that refutes this portrayal. These underlying
traditions shatter the Christian description of Jesus and reveal him as a
man who had accepted the values of his people and who shared the hope
of Israel's messianic deliverance from Rome. Jesus was a Jew in flesh and
spirit.

The attitude of the Messiah Jesus toward Jewish Law was that of
reverence. Jesus preached that he had come not to destroy but to fulfill
the Law and prophecies contained in Isaiah and Jeremiah, that the Jewish
people had to adhere in the strictest sense to the Ten Commandments of
Jewish Law and that if a Jew strictly adhered to this cardinal summary, this
was a good indication that he was destined to participate in the felicities of
the Kingdom of God. To Jesus the Ten Commandments were sacred: they
were the inspired word of God. [1]

Accordingly, the refusal of Jesus to quality his faith in this aspect
of Jewish Law indicates that he had not imagined himself to be God
incarnate. There can not be a shadow of a doubt about this, since the first
commandment of the Law was monotheism which excluded the notion of
a divine trinity in which the Messiah was the Second Person. Had Jesus
lived to read the Gospels, he would have considered the way in which he
was described totally inconsistent with his conception of God. For Jesus
the Lord his God was one God. [2]

Most clergymen are not even familiar with these passages, and if they
are confronted with them by a member of their congregation they usually
sidestep the issue by insisting that faith is what is important. As Paul might
have remarked "do not trust in your own good judgment or fall victim to
logical conclusions." It usually ends there. [3] But what both parties have

missed is that the entire universe and its inhabitants conform to logical designs. Why is Christianity to be given special treatment? Why are its doctrines and history not subject to logical analysis? Take, for instance, the above mentioned teachings of Jesus about his commitment to the Ten Commandments. The logical conclusion of these teachings is that he was s good Jew who would have believed that it was irresponsible for any man to call himself the God of the Heavens and Earth. But for the clergyman and his congregation this could never be so, because the Church teaches the contrary. It is as if the Church knows more about what Jesus taught than he did.

Not only is it irresponsible to say that Jesus considered himself to be God, but it is also foolish to claim that he was really more than a Jewish Messiah. Jesus was proclaimed the Messiah by his followers, and to their way of thinking there was only one kind of Messiah, the Messiah of Israel. This was the gospel underlying all the Gospels. This was the ultimate conviction of the earliest Palestinian traditions about Jesus. It was the conviction contained in this passage: 'Do not give to dogs what is holy, neither cast your pearls before swine, or they will trample them under their feet and turn and tear you.'[4]

I wish to make two remarks about the above-quoted passage. First, it is the consensus of expert opinion today that the allusion in this passage is to the Gentiles. In rabbinical circles especially, swine was a term which denoted non-Israelites.[5] Second, the passage is by no means isolated and therefore unrepresentative of the earliest apostolic traditions about Jesus, since the New Testament contains many such references: 'Do not go to the way of the Gentiles, or to the Samaritan cities: go rather to the lost sheep of Israel.'[6]

Besides the actual teachings of Jesus quoted above, there are also several hints in the Gospels in the form of indirect testimony which support his point of view. In both Mark and Matthew[7] it is vigorously denied that Jesus intended to destroy the Temple as an institution. If Jesus had wanted to disregard Judaism for a new form of religion, there would have been the strongest temptation by him to repudiate worship in the Temple as an indication of a commitment to the Jewish faith. There would have been also the strongest disposition by his followers to say this and reject the Temple. It would have been incumbent upon them to follow a course of repudiation of the Temple, since this form of worship was fundamental to the Jewish way of life. Instead, the twelve apostles, those men who knew Jesus best, continued to worship in the Temple at Jerusalem as devout Jews after his death. This is inexplicable if it had not been firmly established early in the ministry of Jesus that Judaism as a world religion was to be left intact in its essentials. Socially, culturally and religiously this would have been the case. This indirect evidence is invaluable in arriving at a true picture of Jesus. For the actions of his earliest followers mirror what he tended to preach during his brief ministry.

In discussing the Jewishness, so to speak, of the mission and preaching of the Messiah Jesus, we, both writer and reader, must shed two thousand years of conditioning, a disposition resulting from textual or parental indoctrination, which no matter who the inquirer has left some mark. 'Maybe Christianity is a fraud', many a scholar has remarked in the private of his study. 'But if it is, have millions of sincere Christians lived a lie, and died martyrs in vain?' They have allowed these difficult areas to color any investigation of the New Testament period in which they may engage. Admittedly, these are complex questions to confront, let alone answer. But that must not deter us from going on. We have to steadfastly resist any inclination that if Christianity falls in disrepute because of the questions we ask or the answers we obtain it is our fault. Those men who seek the truth can never be labeled destroyers. The truth hurts only those who cannot tolerate it. We bare no responsibility in revealing the eccentricities and preferences of Jesus.

Was Jesus guilty then of Jewish racism? No. While Jesus had directed his preaching to the Jewish people as was expected of the Messiah, he did show on a few occasions an interest in worthy Gentiles. The story of the Canaanite woman, who besought Jesus to help her sick daughter, is a good example of the kind of restricted interest of Jesus. He was at first unwilling to help her daughter, proclaiming with an obvious reference to the doctrine of Israel's divine election:

'I was not sent except to the lost sheep of the house of Israel. But she came and worshipped him, saying, "Lord, help me!" he said in answer. It is not fair to take the children's bread and cast it to the dogs. But she said, Yes, Lord; for even the dogs eat crumbs that fall from their master's table. Then Jesus said her, O woman, great is your faith! Let it be done to you as you wish. And her daughter was healed from that moment.'[8]

Before Jesus treated the woman's daughter, he made it clear that his Messianic proclamation was primarily to the Jews. The Gentiles had no inherent right to share in the coming Kingdom. Jesus was rewarding her for what he saw as her expression of faith in him as God's chosen vehicle of transformation of the existing world order into a Kingdom of righteousness and justice. He was willing, however, to make an exception in the case of a Gentile whose faith was as strong as the Canaanite woman's. When Jesus commended the women 'great is your faith', he surely meant her practical faith in his preaching as the inspired word of God.

Contrary statements have been credited to Jesus in the New Testament. But all these sayings are bogus and reflect what the Church came to believe about Jesus. In the Gospel of Matthew, for instance, it is stated that Jesus commanded his apostles to go forth and preach to all the nations of the world, baptizing them in the name of God the Father, God the Son and God the Holy Spirit.[9] Jesus could never have made this statement, since the original apostles of Jesus actually refused to preach his gospel to non-Jews,[10] and, indeed, St. Paul and the Acts state that the apostles did not baptize in the name of a divine trinity, but in the name of the Messiah Jesus. The Catholic Church historian, St. Eusebius, even argued that the above mentioned Father, Son and Holy Spirit passage was forged.[11]

Those Christians whose job it is to counter a book such as mine can point to several other bogus passages which on the surface support the Church. But none of these sayings credited to Jesus will pass the most rigid test of all. They do not stand up to historical comparisons with other statements and gathered facts which are known to be correct. That is where the Christian interpretation cannot make the grade. It just does not gibe with what a monotheistic Jew was likely to have believed or with what Jesus' earliest followers insisted to be his religious position. It makes all the difference to our understanding of Jesus if this is realized.

In recent years a few scholars have attempted to shed light on Christian Origins, and to an appreciable degree their contributions have been recognized. All credit to these men, but many are Christians and despite their unusual sincerity, they have failed to investigate Jesus in the simpler aspects of his morality. What they have not uncovered, or in some cases refused to admit, is that Jesus was a product of the Jewish spirit, of his time and people. Any contrary conclusion is doomed, because all men are captives of their own age. Jesus was no different. The man Jesus preached

Jewish concepts to Jews in a plainly Jewish environment. What meant all the universe to Jesus was the dramatic recognition by his people. 'You are the Messiah'.

Study Aids

1. Matt. 5.17-19.

2. Mk. 12.28-30.

3. Gal. 2.11-13; Rom.11.13-24; Acts 15.

4. Matt. 7.6.

5. Strack and Billerbeck, Kommentar zum Neunen Testament, 1. pp. 449-500; Grieve, Peake's Commentary in the Bible, p. 707; Black, Aramaic Approach to the Gospels and Acts. Pp. 146-148.

6. Matt. 10.6-7

7. Mk. 14.53-59; Matt. 26.57-61.

8. Matt. 15.24-28.

9. Matt. 28.19.

10. See Chapter 1, Section 2

11. Acts 19.1-6; Euseb., Eccl., bk. 3. Ch. 5.

3

Son of God

'A basic problem for Christianity is that traditionally terms and concepts from the Old Testament have been used without any understanding of what they meant to monotheistic Jesus and his original followers, the men who knew him best, who as we will see during our study repudiated any Christian religion.'

Abram Spiro

The New Testament contains many terms that were used to describe Jesus. They were used by monotheistic Jews who followed Jesus, and they were adopted by heathen Gentiles upon their conversion by St. Paul. This demands no argument. It is the guiding principle upon which any study of these terms is based. It is then the guiding principle that I will use in order to ascertain the relationship between the proclamation of the Messiah Jesus and the most significant term by which Jesus was described in the New Testament, Son of God.

What could a monotheistic Jew in the first century BC mean when he referred to the Messiah as Son of God?

There is no real problem with the above mentioned terminology. In the Old Testament book the expression Son of God is used about many things. Rocks are called Sons of God; trees are called Sons of God; the Jews, themselves, are called Sons of God. The king of Israel, a traditional messianic personality, was also considered a Son of God candidate. And, indeed, St. Paul, in Romans, confirms this very attitude. So we see that this is not uncommon in Scripture.[1]

While the Messiah was never referred to or viewed as God incarnate,[2] he did enjoy Sonship of God. Traditional messianic speculation had linked the Messiah with the King of Israel who became the adoptionist Son of God when God acknowledged his ascension to the royal throne. Had not God told the prophet Nathan as much when he described the mission of King David.

'He shall build a house to my name: and I will establish the throne of his kingdom forever. I will be to him a father: and he shall be to me a son. And if he commit any iniguity, I will correct him with the rod of men, and with the stripes of the children of men. But my mercy I will not take away from him, as I took from Saul, whom I removed from before my face. And they house shall be faithful, and thy kingdom forever before they face: and thy throne shall be firm forever.[3]

The very title Messiah, the Anointed One, or as the specialist would have it God's Anointed, as in the Old Testament books about Saul and David, in Lamentations about Zedekiah and in Isaiah though wrongly extended to the Persian King Cyrus,[4] cancelled out the possibility of divinity. This title was used about more than one man, and, indeed, none of these Messiahs had called himself a god. Messianic Sonship of God obviously signified something entirely different to a monotheistic Jew of the first century than it did to the Gentiles who belonged to the emerging Christian Church.

The Messiah Jesus, therefore, could consider himself the adopted Son of God, since God had acknowledged him as the messianic King of Israel upon his anointing at the River Jordan. Jesus was not the first man now would he be the last to believe that he had communicated with God. Moses, Paul and Mohammed shared a similar belief. Jesus was in good company. But the mission of Jesus was much different than that of those men. He had no new commandments to offer. He had not considered the role of the Gentiles. Jesus had no new religion to preach. God had informed Jesus that he was the Anointed One, that descendant of the house of David whose task it was to make true the prophecies of Israel's messianic deliverance. On that day god had adopted a new David, a son, and Jesus became legitimate, cleansed and born again under unimpeachable conditions. St. Eusiebius of Caesaria, the famous church historian, wrote that this same adoptionist doctrine was adhered to by the twelve apostles and all their followers.[5]

Though the apostles of Jesus confined their preaching to the Jewish people, the mystic Paul extended the mission to the Gentiles. Paul also used the Son of God to describe Jesus when he preached to Gentile communities. And it was in these communities that the term Son of God took on a new meaning. The Gentiles misunderstood this description of Jesus and interpreted it to mean that Jesus was actually God the son incarnate.

The relative ease in which this happened can be understood only if we have an accurate description of the Gentiles. They were for the most part gullible and superstitious.[6] The Romans themselves by the time of Jesus had conjoined the human and divine natures in the person of the Emperor. Augustus Caesar was hailed Divi Fillius or the Son of God by the Senate. The Emperor Gaius Caligula even instituted a temple, with priests and sacrifices to honor his divinity.[7] A later successor to the Emperorship, Domitian, commanded his officials to address him 'Our Lord and Our God'.[8]

When Paul and Barnabas performed what the Gentiles at Lystra considered to be a miracle, the populace thought the gods had appeared in the form of men and hailed Paul the God Mercury and Barnabas Jupiter, God of the Heavens. A priest of the Jupiter cult even brought oxen and garlands to the city and with the people intended to offer sacrifices in honor or Paul and Barnabas. They naturally resisted these sacrifices by telling the Gentiles to abandon these ways and turn to the God of heaven and earth. 'Even with these words', states the author of Acts. 'they could hardly restrain the crowds from offering sacrifices to them'.[9] This kind of thinking obviously had permeated the Empire from the ranks of majesty to those of servitude.

It is no wonder, then, that Jesus, who was called the Son of God and claimed to be a descendant of a royal family as had been the case of the Caesars, was defied. It is not for nothing that in the Gospel of John, Jesus is described in much the same manner as Domitian had insisted 'My Lord and My God'.[10] For it is stated in the Acts that the followers of Paul had accepted another Caesar named Jesus, Son of God.[11]

Study Aids

1. Read Genesis; Rom. 8.14.

2. See Chapter 2, Section 1.

3. 2 Sam. 7. 13-14; Ps. 2. 6-8.

4. The idea of God making a pact with an individual appears often in the Bible.

5. Euseb. Eccl. Hist., bk. 5, ch. 28.

6. Origen, Against Celsus, bk. 1, ch. 9.

7. Suetonius, Gaius, 22.

8. Suetonius, Domitian, 13.

9. Acts 14. 7-19.

10. Jn. 20.28.

11. Acts 17.7.

4

The Rejection,
Execution and
Resurrection of
Jesus

'The Jew Jesus of Nazareth grew up, lived and died among Jewish surroundings. In the night hour on the Cross (between 2 and 3 pm) He spoke the 22nd Psalm. After that He spoke the Sabbath, night and dying prayers of his forefathers. The dying Jew Jesus spoke the same prayers that His Jewish brothers and sisters were to speak during persecutions over fifteen centuries: at the stake, before taking their own lives in the face of their Christian oppressors, in Auschwitz. The Jew Jesus was laid to rest in a grave of honor.

Friedrich Heer

It was not the lower or middle class Jewish people of the first century who rejected the proclamation of the Messiah Jesus and demanded his crucifixion. It was not the Pharisees who had called for criminal procedures against Jesus which would have led to his execution. The Gospel records support his, and as a matter of historical documentation, Jesus possessed all the qualifications that were described by the Pharisees as necessary for a Messiah. It is highly unlikely that the Pharisees and the masses to which they directed their preaching would repudiate a Messiah who fulfilled all their expectations. Guilt as far as the Jewish people are concerned must rest in the hands of only one group.

The distinguished Dr. Heer has come to the proper conclusion, though he was by no means the first expert to do so:

'St. John brands the Pharisees as enemies of Jesus. This is simply not true. During Jesus' lifetime the Sadducees were his enemies – and St. John does not so much as mention them. Jesus moved a great deal in Pharisee circles, and certainly up to AD 62 the Pharisees enjoyed good relations with the leaders of the original church. The disputes between Jesus and the Jews, reported in St. Mark, reflect, without exception, disputes between the later church of the apostles and its social surroundings. They have no place in the historical life of Jesus.'[1]

It was the Sadducees who were responsible for the elimination of Jesus as a messianic contender [2]. They had thrown in their lot with the Romans, and if a Messiah appeared vent on the destruction of the then present world order and restoring the Kingdom of God on earth, the

Sadducees would not have been caught in the middle, a most dangerous position in this case. They could not repudiate their Roman friends in case the Romans were victorious over a Messiah, and they dared not condemn a messianic revolt because they would be placed in the embarrassing position of Jews condemning a Jewish cause that was endorsed by divinely inspired Scripture. The Sadducees advanced the proposition of the condemnation of Jesus to the Romans in an attempt to secure the status quo.

But what charges could the Sadducees have leveled against Jesus that would have impressed the Romans that he was potentially dangerous? Despite what the Gospels say the Sadducees could never have made the charge that Jesus was guilty of blasphemy against the God of Israel and the Heavens. It was well known that reverence of God and his commandments were central features of the ministry of Jesus. This charge would not have interested the Romans anyway, firstly because they did not feel that it was within the Roman province to meddle in the religious affairs of the Jews, and secondly because the Romans, having numerous Gods themselves, were contemptuous of Jewish monotheism. This charge was put in later and reflects the Churches belief that Jesus told everyone he saw that he was God incarnate. No Jew preaching to Jews, believing that he was fulfilling the sacred prophecies and hoping to be acknowledged as the messiah would have been so foolish. The Sadduceen aristocracy had only one offence to charge Jesus with that would have concerned the Romans. They handed Jesus over to Pontius Pilate for persecution and conviction on the charge of criminal subversion. No Roman Procurator could have ignored such a charge.

Jesus was brought before Pilate and the interrogation proceeded in this manner. It is alleged he approached Jesus flippantly and opened with a question that he and Jesus realized was unanswerable. Pilate asked Jesus 'What is Truth?" which has meant something different to all civilizations. He also asked Jesus if he were a king, and Jesus simply threw the ball back to him by saying 'You have said it'. Soon Pilate became tired of this sport. He ordered Jesus to be released at first, then he backpedaled adding a beating, and finally after washing his hands in front of the Sadduceen controlled mod commended Jesus over to the guards for execution. [3]

What made Pontius Pilate condemn Jesus? Two factors probably influenced Pilate's decision. But I must stress that it can never be known for sure which one had the greater weight with Pilate. One of these was the position that Pilate had gotten himself into in regard to the Semitic peoples he governed. More than once he had blundered in his relations with the Jews. He was equally oppressive to the Samaritans. When Pilate was confronted by the Sadduceen controlled mob, perhaps neurotic in his insecure position after reprimands from Rome. He was caught in a dilemma. It was either Jesus or his own career, since if he went against the wishes of the Sadduceen aristocracy and thereby caused another disturbance by freeing Jesus most assuredly these priests would notify Rome and it would endanger his Procuratorship of Judaea. So there was nothing left for Pilate but to get rid of this political hot potato quickly. The charge in the Gospels that Pilate offered the Jews a choice, Bar Abbas or Jesus, as part of the custom of releasing a prisoner each year is poppycock. No statute of Roman law ever existed to support such an act.

The second factor was that Pontius Pilate had second thoughts about Jesus, since he claimed to be the King of Israel, a title that the Jews identified with the Messiah. Unless Pilate was completely ignorant of Israel's hope of national restoration, he would have considered Jesus a serious threat to the security of the Roman Empire: the ultimate goal of the Messiah of Israel was the complete transformation of the existing world order which in this case was Rome. Whether this Messiah was really a man of violence or not had little influence on Pilate. All he could think of was to get rid of Jesus as fast as he could in order to secure the position of the Empire. No less could be asked of any Roman citizen, especially a Procurator who was dedicated to securing peace in the provinces.

Jesus was led up to the Mount and nailed to a cross, bearing the inscription 'King of the Jews'. Jesus responded bravely to the whole business of execution until the end was evident and his hopes and prayers went unanswered. He cried out 'My God, My God why have you forsaken me', an obvious acknowledgement by Jesus that he was not God. [4] It was finished.

Jesus was buried by his friends hours later. All seemed lost. But something happened that was to give new hope to his followers. A story began to circulate that Jesus had risen. The apostles accepted it out of wishful thinking. No one else did. The Gospels contain hints that the Jews claimed the body was stolen. It probably was but not for the reason of perpetuating the story of the resurrection of Jesus. They feared for the safety of the body. These individuals kept still as the belief in the resurrection became disseminated by his apostles and were partially responsible by their silence for the incorporation of a lie into Church records.

Many men still believe that Jesus did rise from the grave. But their belief rests upon the false testimony contained in three of the Gospels. The Gospels credited to Matthew, Luke and John present the resurrection of Jesus as historical and subject to human verification at the time. A careful examination of the circumstances surrounding the resurrection, however, reveals that the earliest account of these events contained in the Gospel of Mark offers no proof that Jesus rose from the dead. [5]

I wish to make two observations about the biblical extracts of the resurrection. First, the earliest account of these events confirms only two things: the tomb was empty and an unidentified man was sighted near the tomb. This man may have been a party to the theft of Jesus' body and was curious to see how his followers responded to the empty tomb. Second, the editors of Matthew, Luke and John found the events as reported in Mark unconvincing. So they added to them. Matthew contains a positive recognition of Jesus. Luke has still another addition with a recognition of Jesus by his uncle Cleophas. John contains the most additions: the principle one is the appearance of Jesus in Galilee.

Many valid criticisms can be made of the post-Marken additions. Two will suffice. First, in Luke, the episode on the road to Emmaus in which Cleophas failed to recognize Jesus until he had departed after spending the entire day talking with Jesus is suspect, since Cleophas was the uncle of Jesus and therefore he would have been familiar with the looks and mannerisms of his nephew. Why then did it take an entire day to recognize Jesus? Second, in John, the additional Galileen appearance is considered to be a textual emendation, since the twenty-first chapter was not part of the original Gospel. [6]

It remains a fact that early in the history of the Church the resurrection of Jesus was accepted as true. Wishful thinking on the part of his followers could not have by itself supported their faith in Jesus very long. Was there anything that might have persuaded Jesus' followers that what happened to him was consistent with the Messiahship? The Old Testament was used in this manner, since it contained passages which alluded to the rejection, execution and resurrection of the Messiah. I have put together some of the passages that could have been used for this purpose.

Rejection

'He is despised and rejected of men; a man of sorrows, and acquainted with grief: he was despised and we esteemed him not.' 'They have spoken against me with a lying tongue.'

Execution

'He was oppressed, and he was afflicted, yet he opened not his mouth: his is brought as a lamb to the slaughter...He was taken from prison and from judgment: and who shall declare his generation?' 'All they that see me laugh to scorn: for dogs have compassed me; the assembly of the wicked have enclosed me.' 'And in my thirst they gave me vinegar to drink...'

Resurrection

'Thought I walk in the midst of trouble, thou wilt revive me: thou shalt stretch forth thine hand against the wrath of mine enemies, and thy right hand shall save me. Then the earth shook and trembled; the foundations of the hills moved and were shaken. After two days will he revive us: and on the third day he will raise us up, and we shall live in his sight.' [7]

To his followers these passages might certify that Jesus was no false Messiah. Jesus had revealed himself as the Messiah, but by some unfortunate mistake he was betrayed and executed for criminal sedition. However, the belief that Jesus rose after three days allowed the apostles and St. Paul to reinterpret the prophecy of Jesus that he would reveal himself as the Son of Man Messiah in his own lifetime to mean that sometime soon after his resurrection he would reappear a second time to establish the Kingdom. This belief caught on in Christian circles, and even today, after almost two thousand years of waiting, the Church still clings to the hope that Jesus will return.

Faith in the resurrection transformed the death of Jesus into an atoning victory for Christians.

Despite the revelations of this chapter many Christians will remain unconvinced that their hero Jesus did not somehow, so to speak, cheat the hangman. Fundamentalists, especially, will not be moved by the facts.

Their refutation will be a telling one in bible circles. All they have to do is to mumble something about being saved. But the chapter was not written for mental deficients. It was never intended for ranters and ravers. Nor did I conceive it my responsibility to attempt to educate the uneducatable. It is my sincere hope that those citizens of the world whose minds are not closed to facts will be moved to pursue this area of New Testament study much further.

Study Aids

1. Heer F., God's First Love, P. 24.

2. Mk. 14.43-65; 15.3032.

3. Mk. 14; Matt. 27; Many biblical scholars really have problems with this alleged dialogue. How could such a conversation become widely known to any popular community? No Roman account existed to substantiate such a claim. No Roman official would have let loose someone so dangerous as Bar Abbas.

4. Matt. 27.46; Again we have a difficult problem. The passage can be interpreted in different ways. Is Jesus making a despairing remark or is Jesus saying he is not God. The answer, in either case, is the same.

5. It is now generally accepted that Mark ends at 16.9 and that there is no account of the resurrection in this Gospel on a par with the others. The oldest MSS do not contain Mk. 16.9-20.

6. Grant, Historical Introduction to the New Testament, p. 159.

7. These Old Testament passages were compiled from several standard texts and in some cases reflect the authors own preference. See Bibliography for Old and New Testament sources used.

SECTION 2

THE RISE OF CHRISTIANITY

'We must be prepared to find the whole drama of the rise of Christianity more confused, more secular, in a word more appropriate to the limitations of its own age.'

F.C. Burkitt

1

The Earliest
Followers of Jesus

'According to the epistles of Paul, the Gospels and the
Acts, the Apostles of Jesus were orthodox Jews who
regularly worshipped in the Temple at Jerusalem;
they carefully observed the ritual requirements of
Judaism; the zeal of these Apostles was to such an
extent that they attracted many priests and Pharisees
to their community' they were described as zealots
for the Law; they demanded that Paul submit
to the ritual requirements of Judaism in order to
demonstrate his orthodoxy;'

The Testament Book

The death of Jesus must have come as a severe shock to his followers.
But their faith was strong: they preached the gospel of Jesus to the Jews,
making Jerusalem their home base. Because of the position in which Peter
is placed in the various lists of the apostles it has always been assumed
that he was the unchallenged head of their community after Jesus dies.
According to the united witness of the New Testament, James, and not
Peter, was the head of the community,. This misconception has to be
cleared up immediately in order that the activities of the earliest followers
of Jesus can be understood. [1]

The Gospels allow us to see only bits and pieces of earlier traditions.
Alone they fail to substantiate conclusively the attitude of the apostles toward
Jesus. All is not lost however. Earlier sources and to an appreciable degree
more reliable testimony is available in the epistles of Paul. Unfortunately,
churchmen have failed to grasp the significance of these epistles, preferred
to gloss over them for what they think to be substantiation for doctrines of
the faith. The significance of Paul's writing goes far beyond the traditional
arguments about Gentile observance of the Law. Such issues are secondary
when compared to what Paul wrote to his followers at Galatia:

'I marvel that you are so soon removed from him that called you into
the grace of Christ to another gospel: Which is not another; but there are
some who trouble you, and they would pervert the gospel of Christ. If any
man preaches any other gospel to you than the one you have heard, let him
be damned.'[2]

Paul recognized the existence of two radically opposed interpretations of the faith. The persons of the other interpretation were most assuredly the apostles of Jesus at Jerusalem. These men were not a small band of Jewish extremists, but a force to be reckoned with attested to by the concern of Paul and his deliberate vagueness as to who these men were. If these men had been the leaders of an irresponsible sect, Paul could have easily repudiated them as the epistles show he often did in such cases. Instead, he referred to them in an obscure way, suggesting an embarrassment about their identity. It is therefore reasonable to conclude that the apostles of the other gospel were men whose authority Paul could not openly question.

The existence of two radically opposed interpretations of the faith of Jesus is therefore obvious. This particular point does not have to be pursued any further. There is one question, however, that is intricately linked with the above mentioned conflict: What were the positions of the apostles and Paul in regard to the messianic faith?

It can be argued that the position of the original apostles was that of the Messiah Jesus. Since these men had lived with Jesus for several years, it is most likely that they would reflect the views of the master. However more evidence is available from the New Testament, though it is of an indirect nature. According to the epistles of Paul, the Gospels and the Acts of the Apostles, the apostles of Jesus were orthodox Jews who regularly worshipped in the Temple at Jerusalem;[3] they carefully observed the ritual requirements of Judaism;[4] the zeal of these apostles was to such an extent that they attracted many priests and Pharisees to their community;[5] they were described as zealots for the Law;[6] they demanded that Paul submit to the ritual requirements of Judaism in order to demonstrate his orthodoxy;[7] the persecution of the Samaritan Christians of the camp of Stephen as recorded in the Acts did not affect the apostles who were considered good Jews;[8] St. Eusibius, quoting St. Hegesipphus, reported that St. James, the official spokesman for the community at Jerusalem was considered a more than adequate observer of the nation's sacred faith.[9]

Indirect as this testimony is, it nevertheless paints a picture of the original followers of Jesus that is consistent with the preaching of Jesus that I have revealed in an earlier chapter.

The position of Paul was certainly not particularistic: it was universalistic. Paul believed that the gospel of Jesus should be preached to Jews and Gentiles, regardless of whether Gentiles would accept the Law.

[10] He did realize, however, that while the Jews had an inherent right to share in the coming Kingdom, the Gentiles did not.[11] The men who had followed Jesus throughout his ministry did not hold with this Paulinism.

It is an historical truism that two opposing forces, seeking the same thing, will clash. The apostles and Paul were no different. There are, however two versions to the actual collision between these camps. The first is that the apostles and Paul reached a détente at Jerusalem, at the famous council of Jerusalem reported in the Acts.[12] The second is that the epistles to the Galatians, to the Corinthians and to Titus show that no solution had been reached. One of these versions is patently false.

I favor the second version, since it has already been established that Paul was having trouble with the apostles at Jerusalem. In AD 57, the party of the Circumcision, under the leadership of James the brother of Jesus, and the party of the uncircumcised, under Paul, were still deeply involved. To the Corinthians Paul wrote:

'But I fear, as the serpent seduced Eve by his treachery, so your minds may be corrupted and fall from a single devotion to Christ Jesus. For if he who comes preaches another Christ whom we did not preach, or if you receive another spirit whom you have not received, or another gospel which you did not accept, you might well bear with him. For I regard myself as in no way inferior to the great apostles of Jesus.'[13]

In the same chapter of 2 Corinthians Paul continued his bitter chastisement of the opposition:

'For they are false apostles, deceitful workers, disguising themselves as apostles of Christ. And no wonder, for Satan himself disguises himself as an angel of light. It is no great thing, then, if his ministers disguise themselves as apostles.'[14]

As late as AD 66, on the eve of the Jewish War against Rome, the pseudo-Pauline letter to Titus shows that to the bitter end there could be no reconciliation between Paulinism and the gospel of the Circumcision.

'For there are also many disobedient, vain babblers and deceivers, especially those of the Circumcision. These must be rebuked, for they upset whole households, teaching things they should not, for the sake of base gain... Rebuke them sharply that they may be sound in faith, and may not listen to Jewish fables and the commandments of men who turn away from the truth... They profess to know God, but by their actions they disown him, being abominable and unbelieving and worthless for any good work.'[15]

It is absolutely inconceivable that a binding decision was made at Jerusalem in AD 50 about the missionary field, since in later documents no decision was known of or adhered to. Paul never once in Galatians or Corinthians mentioned a decision of the Council of Jerusalem in order to justify his preaching 'his Gentile Jesus' to Jews and Gentiles. Apparently the twelve apostles had not even considered that there was another way to correctly preach the gospel of Jesus than the one called Circumcision. Being men of high moral principles and loyal to their masters wishes, they could never let up in fighting the false preaching of Paul. All the New Testament evidence available substantiates this.

At this point I wish to pose a question. Was there inherent in Judaism a rationale that might have made the latter post-War Gentile communities believe that universalism was as much a part of the preaching of Jesus and the apostles as it was Paul's?

It can be shown that there was such a rationale. First, there was numerous passages from the Old Testament which spoke of converting Gentiles to Judaism. [16] Next, the fact that while the apostles refused the faith to anyone who was not a professed Jew, they were willing to allow non-Jews to convert to their faith.[17] Finally, there were passages in the Gospels which indicated that those men and women who would adhere to requirements as describe in point one Jesus was willing to include as potential candidates for the Kingdom of God.[18]

This universalistic rationale, which was incorporated into the New Testament, coupled with the destruction of the original preservers of the faith of the Messiah Jesus, greatly aided the transformation of an essentially particularistic faith into a universalistic religion.

Accordingly, the interpretation of Jesus that Paul repudiated was that of the earliest followers of Jesus. The apostles wanted no part of a religion which was Gentile in orientation. The priority of this apostolic interpretation of Jesus as a true Messiah of Israel must be accepted, since these men had lived with Jesus for several years. They had concluded that the mission of Jesus was consistent with the nationalist tradition of his people.[19]

Study Aids

1. Lk. 24. 13-35; Guignebert, Jesus, pp. 623-24; Acts 12.17; 13-21; 21.18-9.

2. Gal. 1.6-8.

3. Acts 2.46; 3.1;5.12;21.24-26.

4. Acts 10.14; 11.2-3; 15.1; 21.21-24; Gal. 2.11.

5. Acts 6.7; 15.5

6. Acts 21.20.

7. Klausner, From Jesus to Paul, p. 398; Acts 21.

8. Acts 8.1.

9. Euseb., Eccl. Hist. Bk. 2. Ch. 1.2-5.

10. Gal. 2.11-13.

11. Rom. 11.13-24.

12. Acts 15.

13. 2 Cor. 11.3-4.

14. 2 Cor. 11.13-15.

15. Tit. 1.10.

16. See chapters 7, 8, 11 of Isaiah.

17. Gal. 2.

18. See Section 1, Chapter 2.

19. I wish to highly recommend the textual best, easiest to read translation of the testament book, H.J. Schonfield's Authentic New Testament which I relied on for various parts of this work. I have not always agreed with Dr. Schonfield's theories in the past; but with this translation I whole heartedly concur. I must also recommend any of his translations of ancient literature.

2

The Man Paul and 'His' Jesus

'Paul knew that Jesus died a Jew, sharing the ordinary prejudices of Jews, and excluding uncircumcised Gentiles from the blessings of that future kingdom which he went to prepare in heaven. He believed, however, that in being raised by the spirit from the dead he was, in some mysterious manner, promoted to be the savior of all mankind, and became a universalist teacher, bearer of a name of power before which all angels and demons, both in heaven and hell, must prostrate themselves. He died a human being, he was raised a divine life-giving and recreate spirit.'[1]

Frederick Cornwallis Conybeare

Paul is one of the most prominent characters in the New Testament, and his writings represent so much of it that he has been called the true founder of Christianity. There is quite a bit of justification for this statement, since the Christian Religion as it is known today would not exist if had not been for Paul's teachings.

Christianity was in a very primitive state when Paul became one of its champions, an occurrence that was as unexpected as it was disconcerting to the original followers of the Messiah Jesus. Paul had been one of the chief persecutors of early Christians. His conversion was at first thought to be a trick to infiltrate the movement in order to once and for all time destroy the faith. Besides, Paul was so much different in character and background that his presence in the community would be very embarrassing. His activities after that were subject to the greatest suspicions.

This Paul, or as he had been called Saul, came from the city of Tarsus in Cilicia. His family were very strict about his religious upbringing, a fact evidenced by their association with Pharisaism. Tradition has it that at an early age Paul traveled to Jerusalem where he studied under the celebrated Gamaliel. Paul was bright and aggressive, subject to severe moods of depression and anxiety and apparently afflicted with epilepsy. Paul had other negative personality traits too. He often through common sense out the window; his temper was frequently ungovernable; his judgment was erratic and he was possessed with a morbid and inconsistent sense of right and wrong. Paul also entertained thoughts that he had been designated by God for a very special mission, and this tended to over stimulate his curiosity in regard to matters of the occult, perhaps hoping to make himself worthy of God's trust. This might go a long way in explaining Paul's style of preaching.

Paul's early studies had a great influence on his concept of Jesus as Messiah and Son of God. According to his epistles to the Ephesians, Philippians, Cossians, Romans and Galatians Paul had delved into areas that were restricted to only the most learned Pharisees. To the Galatians he stated: 'And I advanced in Jedaism way beyond many contemporaries of my time: since no one has been more anxious than I to grasp the traditions of the ancients'. To the Corinthians he further insisted that he was familiar with 'all mysteries and secret lore'. Like many Pharisees he had studied the Lore of Creation, a branch of Jewish occultic study that dealt with man's relationship with God in creation, which may have lead him to explore the concept of the Two Messiahs, one heavenly archetype Messiah and the other his earthly counterpart who would appear to herald the coming Kingdom. [1]

Paul's teaching concerning the coming of the Messiah was very similar to what these select Pharisees studied. But Paul did not accept the existence of the Two Messiahs in the true sense. He taught that the heavenly Messiah was the sole Messiah, who had temporarily reduced himself to a purely human condition in order to achieve redemption for mankind. To Paul Jesus was only a temporary manifestation of this heavenly Messiah. For this reason Paul was never really interested in the Jesus if history. He stated this emphatically to the Corinthians: 'From now one we know no one in the physical sense. Even if we knew the Messiah in the physical sense, we do no longer. If anyone is in the (heavenly) Messiah his is a new creation. Old associations have gone by the wayside, replaced by new'. [2]

Paul's lack of interest in the historical Jesus made him obnoxious to the apostles at Jerusalem. They deeply resented his highhandedness in proclaiming his version of Jesus as the sole one. This was certainly a slap in the face, since he had never been with Jesus and they had heard him preach for three years and claimed to be successors to his mission and preaching. Their image of Jesus was that of an earthly descendant of King David, that he was the God sent King of the Jewish people and that it was his task at some point in time to initiate the Kingdom of God on earth. Their interpretation centered around an earthly figure and not some spiritual presence as Paul would have it. They probably never understood exactly what Paul meant when he wrote to the Colossians that the Messiah Jesus was:

'The image of the invisible God, the firstborn of every creature. For in him was crated all things in the heavens and on earth, things visible and invisible, whether Thrones or Dominations, or Principalities, or Powers... he is the first before all creatures... he is the beginning, the first born from the dead... For it has pleased God he is the image of God.'[3]

Though Paul preached that the Messiah was crated in the image of God, eh never called him God. On this point only was he in unison with the original followers of Jesus. In his epistle to the Philippians Paul actually denied the divinity of the Messiah:

'Have this mind in your which was also in the Messiah Jesus, who though he possessed godlike form, did not consider himself to be God, but emptied himself, being made like a man. And appearing in the form of man, he humbled himself, being obedient to death, even to death on the cross.'[4]

Since the Messiah of Paul was the firstborn of creation and possessed Godlike form, he could be called the Son of God, though Paul himself firmly committed to the Hebrew doctrine of monotheism was very careful not to go any farther than this description. To Paul there was only One God from whom all things have come and one King Messiah briefly reflected in the earthly presence of Jesus.

If Paul had lived just forty years longer, he would have regarded the way his teaching was interpreted by the Gentiles who heard his message and subsequently composed the Gospels as unjustified. The tritheistic formula of the Gospels is totally inconsistent with Paul's teaching, since he never stated that God was composed of three separate though equal Gods. Now that we comprehend what Paul actually taught we can understand how far off base the Gentiles were when they interpreted the writings of Paul of Tarsus.[5]

Study Aids

1. Gal. 1.14.
2. 1 Cor. 8.2
3. Col. 1.15-22.
4. Phil. 2.5-11.
5. 1 Tim. 2.5; 1 Cor. 8.6.

3

The Jewish War

'It is impossible for us nowadays to realize the shock of AD 70 to a community in which Jewish and Gentile members alike had been reared in the profoundest veneration of the immemorial sanctity of the Holy City and the Temple.'

Burnett Hillman Streeter

Historically speaking, Jews and Christians are abysmally ignorant about the Jewish War against Rome (AD66-70). Quite commonly, for instance I am asked why it took place and what effect it had on the rise of Christianity. This chapter is concerned with partially answering these questions, and the following chapters will deal with this same subject in more detail.

The Jewish War was the product of the historical circumstances from the fourth through the seventh decades of the first century AD in which the Roman Empire, its emperors, legates and legions, seemed to the Jewish people of the abomination describe din the book of Daniel, reminiscent of the tyranny of Antiochus Epiphanus.

From the sources of information about this period, namely the pre-Roman Jew Josephus and the Apocalypses, the Romans did very little to placate the Jews, since the most inept and morally questionable men were chosen as governors and procurators, and, indeed, the political and religious oppression that attended the reigns of these fools stimulated the resentment of the Jewish people. Pious malcontents preached wrath and judgment. Others resorted to murder and brigandage.

The Apocalypse of Baruch, composed about A.D. 60, describes far better than I can the hate Jews held for Rome:

'For that time will arise which brings affliction; for it will come and pass by with quick vehemence, and it will be turbulent coming in the heat of indignation... And there will be many rumors and tidings not a few, and the works of portents will be shown, and promises not a few will be recounted, and some of them will prove idle, and some of them will be confirmed... And whilst they are mediating these things, then zeal will arise in those of whom they thought not, and passion will seize him who is peaceful, and many will be roused in anger to injure many, and they will rouse up armies in order to shed blood.'[1]

It is no wonder that when war broke out few were surprised.

War with Rome was a foolhardy proposition for the Jews from the beginning. Josephus attempted to convince them that such an undertaking was suicidal, since the Romans had a massive superiority in men, money and materials. The Jews refused to listen to reason and the slaughter began in AD 66.

Four years later the Jewish War against Rome ended, though certain fanatics continued the hostilities at Masada until AD 73. The Romans did not take the affair lightly and initiated an era of oppression that ranks among the most severe in the history of mankind. According to Josephus over one million Jews were killed at Jerusalem during the final siege. Of those who survived AD 70, most of them ended up in Roman arenas; the rest starved.[2]

The effects of this Jewish War on nascent Christianity were dramatic. Not only was the focal point for the faith destroyed when Jerusalem was leveled, but many articles of faith were obscured. Many men appeared, espousing new articles of faith that were to alter the development of Christianity profoundly. The Jewish War was, indeed, a turning point in the rise of Christianity, since before the War the movement was decidedly Jewish and after AD 70 it became predominantly Gentile.

Study Aids

1. Apocalypse of Baruch, 48.31-39.
2. Jos., <u>Wars</u>, bk. 6. Ch. 5; bk. 7. Ch. 5.

4

Mark, Matthew and Luke

'Almost all our information about Jesus is found in the four Gospels bearing the names of Matthew, Mark, Luke and John – though these were almost certainly not their real authors. Who their authors, the evangelists, were cannot now be determined; the Gospels themselves probably reached their final form between thirty-five and sixty-five after Jesus' death. The essential "riddle of the New Testament" is the problem of deciding which portions of the Gospels refer authentically to the career and teaching of Jesus, and which, on the other hand, are subsequent additions or inventions by the evangelists, in the light of such intervening events as the development of the rising church and the First Jewish Revolt against the Romans.'

-- Michael Grant

The New Testament contains three Synoptic Gospels, and they were composed as a response to the urgent circumstances which confronted nascent Christianity after the Jewish War. Since the chief apostles of Jesus, his brother James, Peter, and the sons of Zebedec were executed either shortly before or during the War and the lesser ones were scattered and perhaps met violent ends soon after AD 70, all contact was severed between the preservers of the original messianic faith of Jesus at Jerusalem[1] and the Gentile communities. Mark, Matthew and Luke had to fill the gap.

The careful reader may have wondered why I went against tradition when referring to the order of the Synoptic Gospels in the previous paragraph, since most editions of the New Testament list the order of composition of the Synoptics as Matthew, Mark and Luke. Two reasons are offered by clergymen for this order: Eusebius asserted in his *Ecclesiastical History* that Matthew composed the sayings of Jesus in Hebrew an the others copied as they could;[2] and the fourth century Saint Augustine[3] insisted that Mark was a cheap edition of Matthew. However, careful investigation into the formation of the Gospels history by nineteenth century German scholars, namely, Weisse and Wellhausen[4], has shown that this tradition is false.

One cogent argument which New Testament historians employ in favor of the priority of the Gospel of Mark is the obvious dependency of Matthew and Luke upon Mark for material. The authors of Matthew and Luke reproduced the majority of the textual material and ninety percent of the actual words used in Mark.[5] These authors also reproduces the relative order of occurrences and sections as contained in the Gospel of Mark.[6] Accordingly, if Matthew and Luke copied Mark, Mark antedated Matthew and Luke.

Mark, Matthew and Luke, better known as the Synoptic Gospels, were composed by men who did not know Jesus and are roughly dated between AD 90 and 110. All claim to be by the author for whom the Gospel was named. All three authors composed their Gospels outside Palestine, and the majority of their readers were non Jews. The Synoptics were meant to be biographies in which the authors attempted to produce a logical and coherent story of Jesus. They resulted because the authors were concerned with formulating lives of Jesus that would develop inspiration for early Christians. They were also concerned that belief in the Imminent Second Coming of Jesus was falling by the wayside. One of the attestations to the earliness of the Gospel of Mark is that a lack of faith in the Second Coming in the least prominent.

The first Gospel has always been credited to John Mark. He was a nephew of Paul's companion Barnabas, and he accompanied them on their first missionary journey to Cyprus. In the epistles from Rome, Mark is described as though he had aided Paul and was acquainted with some of his teachings[7]. According to Eusebius, a few years after Paul was executed at Rome, Mark composed a life of Jesus.[8]

When Mark wrote his Gospel he had to be very careful about what statements he attributed to Jesus and his followers and how he described the Jewish and Roman attitudes toward Jesus, for Mark was writing in post-war Rome and resentment was very high there regarding sectarian groups.

In keeping with this policy Mark made every attempt possible to disassociate Jesus from Jewish political Messianism. He denied the Davidic descent of the Messiah Jesus[9]. Mark covered up the membership of the Lord's apostle Simon in the militant Zealots by substituting the Aramaic term Cananaean for Zealot when the described him[10]. He instituted the anti-Semitic fraud that the Jewish people had rejected the Messiahship of Jesus and were criminally responsible for his death[11]. And Mark makes Pontius Pilate decree that Jesus represented no threat to the Roman Empire[12].

The works of the first century Jewish historian Josephus were also used by Mark to invent the character Joseph of Arimathea in order to show the post-War Roman officials who might read is Gospel that Pilate was rather sympathetic to Jesus and his followers. Mark made Joseph a follower of Jesus and a member of the Sanhedrin. It is also stated that his mother was present at the triple execution of Jesus and two others. Joseph proceeded to Pilate and requested the body of Jesus after it was all over. Pilate agreed. Jesus was transferred to a close by tomb owned by Joseph where he was put to rest. It has always been a matter of great concern that his Joseph came and went so quickly in the Gospel history.

From an early date, scholars have doubted the likelihood of the person Joseph of Arimathea. In the Greek version of Mark the name is Joseph apo Arimathias, and this came from Josephus' account of his ancestry where he mentioned that his grandfather Joseph begot Matthias which in the Greek translation is Josephou Matthias. The parallelism is marked.

That is not all: there is even a stronger similarity between Josephus and Mark in the case of the appeal to Pilate for the body of Jesus. It seems that Josephus discovered that three of his friends had been crucified after the Jewish War. He approached his friend the Governor Titus and requested their bodies for burial. Interestingly enough, when the bodies were removed from the crosses, one of his friends was still alive and later recovered. This is almost to the sentence a copy of Mark's version. All that had to be done was to change Josephou Matthias to Joseph apo Arimathias and make the sole survivor of a triple crucifixion Jesus.

By requisitioning the character Joseph of Arimathea from the works of Josephus Mark was able to fabricate a positive relationship between Roman officialdom and those who supported Jesus. Matthew and Luke caught on to what Mark had done also copied from Josephus.

Mark also believed that his description of Jesus and his followers as politically impotent would be enhanced if he allowed certain early tradition about Jesus to be put into his Gospel that portrayed him in a derogatory manner. The following will serve as good examples. In his youth the mother of Jesus and his brothers and sisters thought he was insane.[13] When Jesus cursed the fig tree, he displayed totally irrational behavior,[14] It was a pitiful spectacle when Jesus with some twelve followers declared himself the messianic King of Israel.[15] On certain occasions Jesus was unable to perform miracles[16]. Early tradition could not substantiate the resurrection of Jesus.[17]

Something has to be said in mitigation of Mark. Ancients did not believe that literary distortion was bad if it was done for a good cause. Mark's cause, most probably, was to save the Christian community at Rome from the inevitable consequences of the post-War roman policy of hunting down and executing all subversives and descendants of King David.[18] He realized that witch hunts do not always cease when the principles are apprehended and often spill over to include their followers. Mark took no chances when he related the first life of Jesus.

Accordingly, Mark made nascent Christianity temporarily palpable to the Roman Empire. From the time of Mark's Gospel, composed about A.D. 90,[19] until about AD 95, no systematic persecution of Christians was pursued by the Romans.[20] It was not until later in the reign on Domitian (AD 81-96) that Christians, predominantly in the East, were persecuted on a large scale.[21] Conceivably, the Emperor Domitian had read the Gospel of Matthew, composed about AD 95, and was appalled to see that Christianity in the East differed considerably from Roman Christianity in the West.[22] Besides, Matthew contained the bogus revolutionary passage "Think not that I have come to bring peace. I have come to bring a sword."[23]

In the Gospel of Mark another change in the description of Jesus is noticeable: he is referred to as God incarnate. But Mark had nothing at all to do with this; since by the time this Gospel was composed Christianity had become a largely Gentile movement and had absorbed many of the superstitions of the pagans. They had transformed Paul's Jesus from Son of God to God the Son and thought nothing of it. Mark innocently inherited and transmitted what the Gentile Christians came to believe about the Son of God.[24]

Canonical Mark was unique, since no other before John Mark had attempted to compose a life of Jesus. Mark's version became the model on which all future lives of Jesus would be based.

Soon after Mark gained currency other Gospels came into popular circulation. In the beginning they were loyal to what Mark had set down on paper, but eventually the author's imaginations began to run wild. Because the first three Gospels were credited to either apostles of Jesus or followers of these apostles they were considered unimpeachable sources about Jesus. It is interesting to note that by AD 150 numerous Gospels appeared attributing all kinds of doctrines to Jesus that even the early Church had to later repudiate. It shows how far out of hand the situation became. Many early saints mentioned these Gospels, often quoting them as divinely inspired records about the activity of Jesus, his family and apostles. As time passed, all but the four Gospels were put aside by the Church, though here and there aspects of doctrine contained in them were incorporated. Examples of this are some of the oldest tenets of the Roman Catholic Church. In the pseudo Book of James, for instance, the author sought to explain the rather complicated question 'How could Mary and Joseph have several other children besides Jesus if Mary was a perpetual virgin?' The author smoothed over the issue by stating that the other children were by a previous marriage of Joseph.

When Matthew and Luke were composed, in all probability at Alexandria and Corinth respectively, Mark was of course their major source. It is obvious from reading Matthew and Luke that the authors had swallowed to a large degree Mark's version of nascent Christianity. But they did not cast off certain Jewish traditions about Jesus. These traditions were worked over and subordinated to Mark's Roman version so that there would still be a strong appeal to Gentile communities. Sayings of Jesus were retained in Matthew and Luke limiting the mission and preaching of Jesus and the twelve apostles to their native Israel, commanding an observance of Jewish Law and endorsing the doctrine of a purely Jewish Messiah.

Gentile oriented doctrines were also incorporated such as a stronger emphasis on the divinity of Jesus, a Trinitarian formula and a positive universalism. Matthew and Luke would at least on the surface successfully harmonize some of the opposing traditions about Jesus for many early Christians.

The second Gospel to be composed was Matthew. But the name is deceiving; for the Lord's apostle Matthew had nothing to do with its composition. No follower of Jesus would have to rely on Mark for at least seventy percent of his material.[25] No Jew would have interpreted Zechariah 9:9 as related to the entry of Jesus into Jerusalem 'mounted on an ass and a colt, the foul of an ass.' No Jew would have misunderstood Isaiah 7:14 to mean Mary was a virgin and that Immanuel referred to the divinity of Jesus. No Jew would have claimed that Jesus uttered the passage 28:19. Nor would any Jew have interpreted the passage 16:15-19 in the same way the author of the Gospel did.

The author of Matthew continued Mark's policy of pilfering Josephus for material to fabricate or embellish stories about Jesus. The most notable example is the account contained in the final chapter of Matthew of the descending of an angel clothed in white at the tomb of Jesus whose appearance startled the guards to the point of motionlessness. The author developed this version from a description by Josephus of the attempted escape of a Jewish subversive after Jerusalem was leveled. One Simon bar Giora, convinced that he could outwit the Romans, dressed up in a white cloak and appeared out of the ground where the temple had stood. The men who witnessed this were startled and remained motionless. In Matthew Simon became an angel and the crowd that witnessed his attempted escape was transformed into Roman guards.

Another characteristic of the Gospel of Matthew is that early traditions in Mark about Jesus that described him in a derogatory manner or set limitations to his ability were systematically eliminated by the author. The charge that Jesus was insane is absent from Matthew. When in Mark it is stated that 'Jesus healed none of the sick', the version in Matthew is 'Jesus healed all the sick'. In Mark when Jesus is called 'Good' he answers, 'Do not call me good. Only God is good.' Matthew's version said 'Why ask me? God is the one who is good.' Mark's account of Jesus' experience with the fig tree is quite different from Matthew's. Mark states that 'Jesus cursed the tree' and that is all. Matthew contains an addition 'And immediately the fig tree died.' In Mark there is no positive witness to Jesus' resurrection. Matthew has several. The author certainly cleaned up Jesus.[27]

I wish now to shift to the Gospel attributed to Luke. This Gospel was composed about AD 110, and it is considered to be one of the most beautiful pieces of literature that had been produced. It is really too bad that such a masterful literary accomplishment as Luke is historically worthless. Luke suffers the same fate the French have assigned to women and translation.

The tendencies of the Gospel of Luke are as follows. The author is even more apologetic than Mark and Matthew about Jesus in relation to Roman officialdom. He drastically abridged or changed accounts of violent actions on the part of Jesus. He proceeded to describe Jesus as a more humanitarian figure, curing and preaching because of a deep conviction to the doctrine of the brotherhood of mankind, he played up the Second coming of Jesus, perhaps as a result of a certain degree of disparity on the part of many Christians. By making these changes, the author of Luke polished off the rough edges of Mark and Matthew.

A well read man must have composed this third Gospel. Luke's author, as the authors of Mark and Matthew had done years before, took much of his materials from works that were not in popular circulation. Josephus, for instance, was also the source of some of his material. The author of Luke lifted the story of Jesus' youthful wisdom at the Temple and his version of the genealogy of Jesus almost to the sentence from the works of the pro-Roman Jew. Another work that was used by the author of Luke was the *Metamorphoses* by Apuleius. The story of Jesus' appearance to his uncle Cleophas as a prime example of literary theft from Apuleius.[29]

The author of Luke ransacked the Old Testament also and incorporated many stories from it in much the same manner that he used Josephus and Apuleius. Parts of his version of the early life of Jesus and John the Baptist came right from the first and second books of Samuel. The old man Simon was really the aged priest Eli in 1 Samuel 2:22, and his wife Anna was conceived because Samuel's mother was so-called. The age of Jesus when he began to preach reflects the account of David in 2 Samuel 5:4. The Baptist's mother Elizabeth was really Anna of 1 Samuel 1:1-11. And the song she sang in thanks for the birth of John was a rehash of 1 Samuel 1. The authors use of these Old Testament passages added a considerable degree of elucidation and color to the early years of Jesus which otherwise would have remained a blank record, since no other Gospel had any comparable information about the childhood of the Messiah Jesus.[30]

With the completion of the analysis of the Gospel attributed to Luke, we bring our study in this chapter of the purposes and tendencies of Mark, Matthew, and Luke to a close. Despite the many distortions evident in the Synoptics it must be conceded that they turned out to be a powerful influence for the preservation of Christianity. They were pillars of fortitude for adherents. They preserved sufficient material so that the movement would be assured a future.

One more thing has to be cleared up. It is often said that the Gospels are racist statements that have been used by anti-Semitics throughout the centuries.

I do not think there is a good case that the Synoptics, Mark, Matthew and Luke have been a force for anti-Semitism. But there is a villain! The Gospel of John or often called the Fourth Gospel fits the bill. Its nature totally contradicts the other three. In John, Jesus makes blatantly anti-Semitic statements. I believe that Dr. Freidrich Herr, Professor of the History of Ideas at Vienna University and editor of Die Furche, and himself a Roman Catholic, has tried to set the record straight:

'The Gospel of Jesus Christ, the 'Good News' of the Redeemer, became for millions of Jews the messenger of death. Millions of Christians have based their hatred of the Jews on it, have taken it as a call to destroy or at the least enslave the Jews, 'the people who killed Christ'. Are the Gospels the indestructible cell from which new life stems for Christians – and death for Jews? Do they preach an anti-Semitism on which Christians and anti-Christians can legitimately draw to this day?... The fourth Gospel, the Gospel according to St. John, is the most pro-Roman and anti-Jewish of them all. It is also furthest away in time from the historical Jesus. The Gospel according to St. John takes the theological argument that the Jews have been the enemies of Jesus right from the beginning of time, coming straight from the Devil. St. John's thinking owes something to Gnosticism (a fact that is very often denied): all men belong either to the realm of the Devil or the realm of Light. St. John was certainly basing himself on Qumran writings. These Jewish sectarians, escaping to the desert, described themselves as 'children of the Light'. Their Jewish enemies, triumphant in Jerusalem, were in their eyes 'children of Light'; Catholics, heathens and Communists are 'children of Darkness'... St. John's portrait of Jesus was separated by more than a century from Jesus of Nazareth, the son of Mary. His Christ is no longer a Jew, hardly even a human being, but rather a prince of Light, 'the true light', a cosmic world leader who triumphed over the powers of Darkness. This majestic Christ did not concern Himself with sinners, like the Jesus of the three synoptists. The words repentance and conversion appear nowhere in St. John... The Jews belong to the damned. The synagogue is a synagogue of Satan.'[31]

That hate is the product of divine inspiration should be repugnant to all decent people in our democracy with a "Bill of Rights".

Study Aids

1. Brandon, S.G.F. <u>Fall of Jerusalem and the Christian Church</u>, ch. "Jewish War Against Rome".

2. Euseb. <u>Eccl. Hist.</u>, bk. 3, ch. 39.

3. Streeter, B.H., <u>Four Gospels</u>, pp. 157-8.

4. Wellhausen, J., <u>Einleitung in die drei ersten Evangelien</u>, where it is studied in detail.

5. Op. Sit. Street, pp. 159-60

6. Op. Sti. Streeter, pp. 160-1.

7. Col. 4. 10-11.

8. Euseb. <u>Eccl. Hist.</u>, bk. 3, ch. 11.

9. Mk. 12:35-37.

10. Mk. 3:18; 5:41; 7:34; 15:22; 15:34.

11. Mk. 14:43-65; 15:14.

12. Mk. 15.

13. Mk. 3:21.

14. Mk. 11:12-14.

15. Mk. 15:2.

16. Mk 6:5-6.

17. Mk. 16:1-8 is all that is contained in the oldest MSS.

18. Euseb. <u>Eccl. Hist.</u>, bk. 3.

19. This date is contrary to the course of scholarship in the twentieth century, but it more fits the authors dating of Mark than previous attempts.

20. Euseb., <u>Eccl. Hist.</u>, bk. 3.

21. <u>Letter of Pliny to Trajan</u> (revised by Hutchinson, Leob Classical Library).

22. Rev. 1-21.

23. Matt. 10:34.

24. Grant, R., <u>Historical Introduction to the New Testament</u>, p. 348.

25. Streeter, B.H., <u>Four Gospels</u>, ch. 'Fundamental Solution'.

26. The best defence of these passages is contained in the Encyclopedia Britannica, notably the 1888 edition, whose expert leadership by Robertson Smith proved too scholarly for the Protestant community of the late nineteenth century.

27. Matt. 8:16-17; 19:16-19; 21:18-22; 28:1-20.

28. The Lukan literature is discussed in detail by W.G. Kummel, <u>Introduction to the New Testament</u>.

29. See Robert Graves, <u>Nazorean Gospel Restored</u>, for a discussion of the sources.

30. This subject owed a great deal to the labors of J. Rendel Harries whose scholarship has not been widely appreciated.

31. Herr, F. <u>God's First Love</u>. Ch. 4.

5

New Testament Whoppers

'How can we forgive the supine ignorance of the entire scientific community in the first century?'
- Edward Gibbon

For ancient man, Gentile and Jew, it was commonplace to attribute superhuman powers to sages and legendary heroes. The Roman historian A. Cornelius Tacitus, for instance, credited many miracles to the Emperor Vespasian while at Alexandria en route to Rome about AD 70.

'In the months during with Vespasian was waiting at Alexandria for the periodical return of the summer gales and settled weather at sea, many wonders occurred, which seemed to point him out as the object of the favor of heaven and partiality of the gods. One of the common people of Alexandria, well known for his blindness, threw himself at the emperor's knees, and implored him, with groans, to heal his infirmity. This he did by the advice of the god Serapis, whom this nation, devoted as it is to superstitions, worships more than any other divinity. He begged Vespasian that he would deign to moisten his cheeks and eyeballs with his spittle.'[1]

Because of the above mentioned tendency of ancient commentators, it is easy to understand why many superhuman feats were attributed to Jesus. Jesus may have had a better than average understanding of the healing arts as had most sages of his day. But while he may have become a Lister or a Pasteur had he lived eighteen hundred years later, Jesus was not God. He was, therefore, not capable of changing those chemical and physical laws by which the world is governed.

Despite the facts, the New Testament contains several fantastic stories or whoppers about Jesus' ability to perform miracles. From Mark on through John, Jesus is presented as performing one miracle after another. The authors actually lost sight of the reason for this preaching and substituted a long list of prodigies that made Jesus the first centuries most celebrated magician, stunt man and doctor. These stories are testimony to what can happen when men do not check their imaginations. An ounce of responsibility in these cases would have far exceeded in effect the pounds of cures found in the Gospels. What ability Jesus had as a healer is marred by these ridiculous 'Ned Buntline' whoppers.

The predisposition of the men who composed the Gospels forced them to interpret every unusual act reported about Jesus to be a true miracle that must have been predicted in the Old Testament. This probably involved several steps. The first step in this process entailed the recollection by these men of some incident that was reported to them many years after the death of Jesus. The second step involved the ransacking of the Old Testament for a prophecy that the incident supported. For the final step, the incident and the prophecy would be integrated in the Gospels to present a clear picture of a miracle that Jesus had performed as predicted in the Bible.

The story in Mark of Jesus walking on the water is easily understood.[2] The story is associated with the storm on a lake, Jesus made his apostles cross over by boat, while he departed to a mountain close by to pray. A storm rose, and the apostles were struggling to get near shore, Jesus suddenly appeared to them on the bank. In the dim light these superstitious men took Jesus for the spirit who haunted the nearby shores. These men must have had a sigh of relief when Jesus called out. As he waded in the shallow water he was helped aboard. When he came into the boat the wind subsided.

In reality Jesus walked by the water. Later this was changed to on the water, since the Hebrew form of 'by the water' can also be translated 'on the water'. The anxious author of Mark preferred the more dramatic and totally inaccurate translation. He turned to the Psalms and found an interesting parallel: 'His way is on the waters and the great seas'.[3] No less could be expected of Mark's Jesus, and so the author made Jesus walk on the water.

It has always seemed more of a contradiction than an indication of fulfilled prophecies for New Testament authors to call upon the Old Testament tradition whose conception of a Messiah was so different from theirs or the emerging Christian Church. But at the time they were more interested in fabricating whoppers, sometimes stealing part of one quotation and splicing it with another to gibe with what they wanted to say in the Gospel: in the first chapter of Mark, for instance, verses two and three are attributed to Isaiah when they are really Machli spliced with Isaiah.

A similar process is discernable in Matthew in the story of the virgin birth of Jesus. According to Matthew Mary was found to be pregnant before she was married to Joseph. Joseph became very disturbed because as far as he knew, it was not his child. Things were cleared up when God explained the circumstances of the pregnancy to him. It seems that Mary was to bare the Son of God himself. But God had promised not to violate her body in the usual manner, being that she was unmarried and engaged, and such an act would have been unbecoming of one of his position. Joseph agreed to do the honorable thing, and so he gave Mary's child a legitimate earthly father. The marriage must have solved a lot of problems as far as the neighbors were concerned. [4]

When the author of Matthew came across this rather sensitive story, he realized that it was necessary to clean it up. He thumbed through Isaiah and found: 'Therefore the Lord himself will give you a sign; Behold a virgin will conceive, and bare a son and he will be called Immanuel.' When this prophecy was integrated into the story, it helped to legitimize an otherwise scandalous account by asserting that God's will was fulfilled as dictated in the Old Testament[5]

He failed to point out, however, that the prophet of Isaiah had meant the passage for King Hezekiah and that the proper translation was 'a young marriageable woman will conceive' and not 'a virgin will conceive', since the prophet of Isaiah had used the Hebrew word 'alma' instead of 'bethula'. He also mistranslated the Hebrew form 'Immanuel'. The author jumped at the alternative translation 'God with us', completely ignoring the preferred translation 'God is with us'. Having accepted the doctrine of monotheism by the birth of Jesus, the Jews would have considered the alternative translation blasphemous. The Jews had believed that in the Kingdom to come the presence of the Messiah also meant God was with their cause or 'God is with us'.

Far better than I can, Professor Conybear, almost one hundred years ago, gave a telling scholarly analysis of these famous prophecies described in the book of Isaiah:

'The Jews of the second century, as they meet us in the pages of Justin Martyr (AD 130-150) though he is a hostile witness, yet contrast favorably with the Christians of the age. For they exhibit a higher and purer monotheism, in so far as they condemn as a pagan fable the story of god engendering a son by a mortal woman,. It was, they declare, an echo of the myth of Danae and of her son Perseus, begotten by Zeus in a shower of gold. These second-century Jews were also able to interpret their old prophets in a more critical manner than the Christians. They pointed out, for example, that Isaiah's Hebrew text (Isaiah vii. 14), properly translated, means no more than that "a young girl (or maiden) shall conceive and bear a son"; and the Rabbi Aquila and Theodotion the Ebionite issued now Greek translations, in which the ambiguous Greek word parthenos or virgin was replaced by neanis – a young woman. They thus cut away the ground from under the feet of the Christians, who had, as we have seen above (p. 180), little except prophecy on which to base their legend. Nothing has so much excited the spleen of Christian and Catholic writers as the substitution of *neanis* for *parthenos*. But time has its revenges; and the recent revisers of the English Bible, timid time-servers as they were, yet felt themselves constrained to add at this verse the marginal note, "*or maiden*". For this, and not *virgin*, is the proper equivalent of the Hebrew word *alma*, which indicated not a woman's quality, but her age, so resembling the German equivalent *Jungfrau*. Let us note, in passing, that to the mind of healthy-minded Teutons, a young woman is a virgin, and a virgin a young woman.

The Jews of that early age also showed some faculty in critical exegesis when they had to overthrow Christian beliefs; for they pointed out that Isaiah, in writing his seventh chapter, had in view, not a far-off Messiah, but Hezekiah, their King. It was only towards the close of the last century, began to be adopted by our divines; today no self-respecting Hebraist would venture to suggest that this or any other passage of Isaiah was any prediction of Jesus of Nazareth.'[6]

The Catholic Church was not satisfied with Matthew's account and proceeded to insist that Mary was a perpetual virgin despite all the New Testament evidence to the contrary. Mark contains the testimony that Jesus had brothers and sisters. Matthew supports the obvious connotation of Mark, since it is stated in the genealogy that Mary and Joseph had sexual intercourse after Jesus was born.[7] Catholics have attempted to explain away the brothers and sisters of Jesus by insisting that they were the product of another marriage of Joseph, or failing to prove this, they claim the expression 'brothers and sisters' meant something else. Proof again is lacking. It is surprising what a Papal decree can do for history.

The story in Mark of the stilling of the storm on the Sea of Galilee is simple enough to explain.[8] After teaching almost an entire day from a dingy along the shores of the Sea of Galilee, Jesus was recognizably tired. Upon issuing orders to cross the Sea he fell asleep. A storm arose, but Jesus was not wakened by its fury. To the apostles the storm seemed to get out of control, and in their fear of drowning, they aroused an exhausted Jesus. At the very moment the storm was stilled.

When the author Mark decided to prepare this story for his Gospel, he was not at all concerned that this phenomenon was somewhat common to the Sea of Galilee. The winds will rush through the nearby ravines almost without warning and just as quickly subside. He was more concerned with pilfering the Old Testament until came up with the following prophecy: 'He will still the roaring of the waters and the roaring of their waves and tumult of his people.'[9] Mark would tolerate not less for his Jesus, and so he made Jesus calm the storm as he wakened.

With the final story that I wish to discuss, the raising of Lazarus as related in the Gospel of John, we have perhaps the best example of how unfaithful an author can be to the truth. No doubt some story was reported about a man who had fainted from exhaustion due to a diabetic condition of heat prostration and who appeared to be dead to the superstitious peasant folk. Jesus had happened to be in the vicinity and was called upon to examine the man. After Jesus had administered what has come to be known as first aid, the man regained consciousness.[10]

Men have always been subject to these spells of unconsciousness, and the Judean and Galilean country sides are especially conducive to such conditions. But since everything that happened to Jesus had to have messianic significance and therefore must have been foretold, this was ignored and the Old Testament was given deference. After the raising of Lazarus, or whatever his name was, fulfilled would-be divinely inspired prophecies: 'Though I walk in the midst of trouble you will revive me... God will redeem my soul from the grave... For he will not leave my soul in the grave... He will show me the path of life... After two days he will revive us...' John did the rest for Jesus.[11]

The fact that this story was not even contained in the Synoptics did not bother John. Nor did the fact that objective sources, those outside the Christian community, those scientists who were dedicated to recording all superhuman facts remained totally ignorant of the raising of Lazarus.

Pliny and Seneca, each in an exhausting treatise about nature and uncommon occurrences, did not even hint that the Lazarus healing ever happened. Could the entire scientific community in the first century be so unobservant?[12]

Christians have accepted these stories at face value and their faith has been greatly bolstered by them. For these poor souls, they were proof positive that Jesus was God and that he controlled all human circumstances. It used to be this simple. I doubt very much that these whoppers will still have credibility for most readers after this examination. If their faith remains intact, it will be one devoid of the kind of nonsense that the Church has spoon fed them in the past. Their faith will not be in a kind of carnival creature who does tricks to amuse the masses, but in a man, a man dedicated to the ideal that this world can be a better place to live.

Study Aids

1. Tacit., <u>Annals</u>, bk. 4. Ch. 81.

2. Mk. 6: 45-51.

3. Ps. 67: 19.

4. Matt. 1: 1-25.

5. Isa. 7: 14; Rogers, <u>Abingdon Commentary on the Bible</u>, Article 'Isaiah' p. 643.

6. Some Christian scholars have claimed that while this is correct, the Jews still took it to mean 'virgin'. There is no basis for this assertion. Conyebear F.C., <u>The Origins of Christianity</u> pgs. 208-210.

7. Mk. 3: 21; Matt. 1:25.

8. Mk. 4: 35-38.

9. Ps. 55:7

10. Jn. 11.

11. Ps. 18; Hos. 6.

12. Gibbon, <u>Decline and Fall of the Roman Empire</u>, ch. 25, p. 206.

6

Paul and the Old
Guard

'Had Paul also so known Jesus, his visions could not
so lightly have soared into the ridiculous. His Jesus
would have remained a mere human Messiah of
the Jews. But in that case Christianity would have
fallen stillborn on the world, and have vanished as
it began – an obscure sect of messianically-minded
Jews.'

Abbé Loisy

Having substituted a kind of Heracles character on the Gospel records
in the place of the historical Jesus, it seemed the task to which Mark,
Matthew and Luke had devoted their energy was accomplished. And to
an appreciable degree that is true, but there remained an embarrassing
question that sooner or later would have to be answered. Why had St.
Paul been at odds with the apostles of Jesus, those men who knew him
best, about the mission and preaching of Jesus?

Bolder and more imaginative men rose to the occasion, and 1 and 2
Peter, 1 Clement, the Acts of the Apostles and the Gospel of John were
composed to answer any question that may arise about this sticky subject.

The first two of these documents, 1 and 2 Peter, were written about
AD 115, and purported to be from St. Peter to the Christian communities
of Asia Minor. In the first epistle, Peter, who had actually been hostile
to Paul, is presented as advocating pro-Pauline ideas in regard to Man's
subservience to the Roman Empire. 2 Peter went much farther by directly
endorsing Paulinism:

'Therefore, beloved, while you look for these things, endeavor to be
found by him without spot and blameless, in peace. And regard the long-
suffering of our Lord as salvation. Just as our most dear brother Paul also,
according to the wisdom given him, has written to you, as indeed he did in
all his epistles, speaking in them of these things.'[1]

Clement's epistle to the Corinthians has been the subject of considerable
debate between Protestants and Catholics, since both camps have used
it to prove or disprove the Catholic doctrine that the Pope has always
exercised absolute power over Christendom. Whether or not 1 Clement
supports the Pope's claims, it remains a fact that Clement had a profound
influence on Christianity. Having been incorporated into one of the oldest
collections of Christian literature 1 Clement was an early contributor to

the reconciling of the old with the new, James and Peter with Paul:

'Through envy the most righteous pillars of the community were persecuted and killed. Peter, who on account of his unrighteousness suffered many trials, and having fulfilled his suffering went to heaven. By jealousy Paul showed the way to the prize of endurance... he was thus a herald both in the East and West, he gained the noble fame of his faith, he preached uprightness to the world, and when he completed preaching in the West he gave testimony before the rules of the country, and he passed from the world a great example of endurance.'[2]

About the same time 1 Clement was gaining currency in the Christian communities the Acts of the Apostles was composed, Acts attempted to deal head on with the conflict between Paul and the Apostles. The whole matter is smoothed over by instituting a Council at Jerusalem where the differences were ironed out. The story is a good one on the surface, and it sure fooled the Christians. But its foundation is synthetic, a revelation apparent if the epistles of Paul are read first. Paul's epistles, all of which were written after the Council, contain not the slightest proof of the decision that is contained in the following speech, falsely credited to James:

'Brethren, listen to me. Peter has told how God first visited the Gentiles to take from among them a people to bear his name. And with this the words of the prophets agree, as it is written, 'After these things I will return and will rebuild the House of David which has fallen down, and the ruins thereof I will rebuild, and I will set it up; that the rest of mankind may seek after the Lord, and all nations upon whom my name is invoked, says the Lord, who does these things.' 'To the Lord was his own work known from the beginning of the world.' Therefore my judgment is not to disquiet those who from among the Gentiles are turning to the Lord; but to send them written instructions to abstain from anything that has been contaminated by idols and from immorality and from anything strangled and from blood. For Moses for generations past has had his preachers in every city in the synagogues, where his is read aloud every Sabbath.'[3]

The process of smoothing over any conflict between the Apostles and Paul was completed when the Gospel of John was forged about AD140. No other document offers up so many falsehoods, not the least of which is the meshing together of the Pauline ideas of the messianic archetype Jesus, the Son of God, with the pagan style of oration. While Jesus was portrayed in a totally untrue and blasphemous way in the Synoptics, the editor of John went two steps farther. He made Jesus himself glory in his own blasphemy and to condemn, as Paul had, the sacred Law of Israel. By setting forth a gospel purportedly by Apostle John in which Jesus supports Pauline ideas, some deceitful person made it seem that there could never have been a conflict between Paul and Jesus' followers.

I have on every occasion questioned the veracity of these documents. And there was good reason. 1 and 2 Peter could not possibly have been written by the Apostle Peter, since the advanced ideas expressed and the language used were clearly not those of an ignorant fisherman who the Synoptics report was not even conversant with his own language:[4] besides, the circumstances alluded to – that of violent persecution – did not exist until after the death of Peter.[5]

John, too, was not written by John the son of Zebedee for the simple reasons that the son of Zebedee was killed long before the Gospel was composed, and, experts have proved that more than one man has fiddled with this Gospel.[6]

Much has been written by churchmen about the life of Jesus and first century Christianity, most of which I have revealed as false. Jesus was not God incarnate and his mother was no virgin. Vicious power struggles existed after Jesus was killed between those who picked up his banner. Even the Christian documents which people were accustomed to think of as divinely inspired were actually re-dated and shaped to fit historical necessities. The reconciliation of James and Peter with Paul and the Gentiles mission proved to be just another example of this kind of phenomena.

Study Aids

1. 2 Pet. 3: 14-16.

2. 1 Clem. 5:. 1-7.

3. Acts 15: 13-19.

4. Cranfield, <u>Peake's Commentary</u>, article 'Peter'.

5. 1 Peter 1: 6; 2:12;4: 12-19;5:9.

6. Barret, <u>Peake's Commentary</u>, article 'John'.

7

A Soldier Never
Dies

'The real apostles of Jesus enjoyed thoughts enough
of him after death, but we do not hear that they
invested the figure they saw with the heavenly role
and fantastic attributes of the Pauline version. It is
certain they did not, and could not do so; for they
had known him in the flesh, and were confused by
what Paul described as carnal memories.'

Theodore Harnack

Earlier in the book, in chapter 3 of this section, in referring to the
fate of the earliest followers of Jesus, I stated that they were killed either
before or shortly after the Jewish War against Rome. And in the broadest
sense that is true. It is known that the sons of Zebedee were killed before
the war. James the brother of Jesus was martyred by the Sanhedrin about
AD 62; Peter was crucified in AD 64; and Paul was put to death during
the hostilities. But what happened to the others, Matthew, Andrew, Philip,
Bartholomew, Thomas, Thaddaeus Simon? How long after AD70 did
they survive? Why is there no favorable mention of them by Christian
communities after the Jewish War? Surely these men, the seven surviving
members of that elite group who knew Jesus intimately, would have been
prizes for any community to boast about. But none did. An extract from St.
Eusebius, paraphrasing Hegesippus, the second century Christian writer,
may begin to shed some light on this matter:[1]

'After the martyrdom of James, and the capture of Jerusalem which
immediately followed, the report is that those of the apostles and disciples
of Jesus that were yet surviving came together from all parts with those
that were related to Jesus according to the flesh; for the greater part of
them were still living. These consulted together to determine whom it
was proper to pronounce worthy of being the successor of James. They
unanimously declared Simeon son of Cleophas as worthy of the Episcopal
seat there. They say he was cousin of Jesus, for Hegesippus asserts that
Cleophas was the brother of Joseph.'

Does this mean that the apostolic survivors of the Jewish War had still
considered James; and not Paul's to be the only valid interpretation of the
mission and preaching of Jesus. It sure looks that way. Irenaeus seems to
agree with this conclusion:[2]

'They use the Gospel of Matthew only and reject the Apostle Paul, maintaining that he was an apostate from the Law. As to the prophetical writings, they endeavor to expound them in a somewhat singular manner; they practice circumcision, persevere in the observance of those customs which are enjoined by the Law, and are so Judaic in their way of life, that they even adore Jerusalem as it were the House of God.'

What we have here is unimpeachable evidence from a Western Christian that a rift still existed between those inheritors of the preaching of Jesus and the Gentile communities. When Irenaeus referred to Matthew's Gospel he did not mean the canical gospel attributed to Matthew with its Pauline tendencies, but a Hebrew version which he called the 'Oracles', in many respect much like the Toldeth Jeshu or parts of the Gospel according to the Hebrews. The Hebrew oracles compiled by Matthew probably included no more than sayings of Jesus with a strong Jewish flavor and Davidic genealogy. This evidence goes a long way in explaining the refusal of Gentile communities to mention the remaining apostles.

The fate of the remaining apostles still seems obscure and especially the approximate dates of their demises. Eusebius must again be consulted:[3]

'Down to the invasion of the Jews by Hadrian (AD 132) there were fifteen successions of bishops (of Jerusalem) all of whom, they say, were Hebrews from the first and received the knowledge of Jesus pre and unadulterated... For at that time the whole Church under them consisted of faithful Hebrews, who continued from the time of the apostles (James, Simeon, Justus, Zaccheus, Tobias, Benjamin, John, Matthew, Philip, Seneca, Justus II, Levi, Ephraim, Joseph and Judas) until the siege which then took place.'

There seems to be no reason to doubt Eusebius testimony. But he really accounts for only two of the apostles, Matthew and Philip, John and Judas mentioned above cannot possibly be those men of the gospel story. Our limited experience is ultimately going to force us to conclude that the date of the second Jewish War against Rome AD 132-5 quoted by Eusebius must be the last possible date that can be assigned to the death of the apostles. There have been cases reported of men living to advanced ages. So it is possible, though it does at the same time stretch ones imagination.

It is obvious now that Catholic Christianity must have kept close tabs on the surviving apostles and their converts, since the chief historians of the Church, Eusebius, Hegesippus and Irenaeus compiled somewhat detailed records of their actions. It was incumbent upon them to follow this course. It must have been embarrassing to the early Catholics that the original followers of their master Jesus insisted that Catholicism was a heresy. Because of this each and every attempt of those surviving apostles to show how false the Catholic version of the faith was had to be known of in order to have an opportunity for a counter argument. No attempt was ever made by the Catholics to explain why there was an unbroken chain of successors from James up until AD 132 who had bitterly repudiated Western Christendom. Time would come to the aid of the Catholics, since all the remaining apostles eventually passed on, and the second Jewish War provided the means for the destruction of many of their converts. It remains a historical fact, however, that for several hundred years there were adherents to the apostolic interpretation of Jesus.

74

Study Aids

1. Eusebius, <u>Eccl. Hist.</u>, 3. 10. 16.
2. Irenaeus, <u>Against Heresies</u>, 1.26., 1.5.
3. Euseb. <u>Eccl. Hist.</u>, 3.3.7.

8
The Christian
Church

'This (forged) document (Pseudo-Clementine Epistle of Clement to James) was used in almost every Papal communication in the Middle Ages as the justification for Papal power.'

Walter Ullmann

The Christian Church, as it is presently constituted, with its God-man, champion Jesus, and an entire edifice of dogma based upon his divinity, bares little resemblance to the preachments of the historical Jesus. The Jesus of history was a monotheist; while the Christian Jesus was a tritheist. The Jesus of history was a purely Jewish Messiah; and the Christian Jesus was a Universalist. The historical Jesus died at the crucifixion; while the Christ of Christianity died a god.[1]

It makes all the difference if Jesus is viewed as man and not God, since he can therefore be examined both for what he was and for what he was made to be. Perhaps the greatest value of this book has been for the reader to see how historical circumstances can give rise to drastic change to the image of a man or to some concept associated with him. The change that Jesus underwent in the New Testament resembles the evolution of the American Presidency, since presidential power, as it was constitutionally defined in the eighteenth century and as practiced up to 1932, has little resemblance to the power exercised by President Richard Nixon.[2]

Inevitably, the question will be asked: How did the Christian Church develop so rapidly after the Jewish War?

I have selected two circumstances as contributing to the growth of the Church. The first of these was the existence and strategic location of a largely Gentile community in Rome. Since the community was, at least for a considerable time anyway, considered harmless by the Romans, it was allowed to exist and flourish. It is not surprising, even considering the persecution of Christians by Domitian, which after three hundred years of touch and go coexistence with the Empire the Church became the State religion of Rome, instituted by the Emperor Constantine.

The second circumstance is closely related to the first. As a result of the relative lack of persecution of the faith in the West, the Roman community was able to develop a quick succession of elders, or, as they were called in the second century, popes, who exercised a great influence over other floundering communities. Consequently, the Roman community became a unifying force for Christendom. This Roman leadership has to be divorced however from the posturing polemical figure of the Pope as exemplified by the Dogmatic Constitution of 1870[3], since there is not one genuine document extant which proves that the early popes of Rome possessed Olympian powers of infallibility or that they were the acknowledged successors of the apostolic community at Jerusalem.[4] One of the oldest documents or the Christian Church, the epistle of Clement to the Corinthians, proves that the early Roman popes were not in the position to command fellow believers in other communities. They served rather as consultants.

Dr. Barraclough, one of the foremost experts on Christian Origins and Papal Supremacy, has made a definitive series of conclusions concerning Catholic claims about the Popa, or Papa:

'In all this there is no indication that the early Christian community in Rome was presided over by a bishop. This again is not surprising. The early Christian churches were small communities, bound together by faith and brotherly love, which had no need for a monarchical head. Within each congregation, no doubt, a few men – distinguished preachers or early converts – stood out as 'elders' and 'overseers'. As 'shepherds' of their flock, they were called indifferently 'bishops' and 'presbyters'; and for the dispensing of alms and other tasks the communities soon appointed deacons and deaconesses. But such authority as they possessed they exercised in common, and it was only in the second half of the second century that the grades in the hierarchy were defined and differentiated and the 'bishop' drew ahead as the appointed leader of this church. In this development Rome was noticeably prominent. Rather it began in the east, and can only be traced in Rome from the time of Hippolytus in the early third century. Nevertheless it is significant that the first lists of the bishops of Rome date from AD 160-85; that they make Peter and Paul conjointly the founders of the Roman church; and that none asserts that St. Peter himself was bishop. Only about AD 220, in the time of pope Callistus, does the practice arise of reckoning Peter as the first bishop of Rome; and it was another twenty or thirty years before the tradition took shape according to which, shortly before his death, St. Peter 'laid hands' upon Clement – who, in the earlier lists, appears in the third place. After Linus and Anencletus – as 'bishop of the Romans' and entrusted him with his 'chair of discourse' ... It is against this background that the raise of the bishop of Rome must be set. The idea of apostolic succession was, of course, in no way identified with Rome. There were many other churches O Jerusalem, Antioch, Ephesus, Smyrna, Philippi, Thessalonica, Corinth – which claimed descent from one or other of the apostles; and Alexandria was not slow to join their ranks by appropriation of Mark as its founder. Irenaues and Tertullian were not arguing on behalf of Rome; their concern was to assert Episcopal authority as such, not papal authority or the authority of the Roman bishop. Antioch and Corinth, as well as Rome, claimed descent from St. Peter. But Rome was the only apostolic church in the western half of the Roman Empire... After Stephen there was little progress in the theoretical formulation of papal right until popes Damasus (366-84) and Leo 1 (440-61). In practice, Stephen's pronouncements had not visible effect. The church, in organization, was still a federation of Episcopal churches, each with its own customs and usages, loosely ruled by synods, and only be straining the evidence can it be argued that any special authority was vested in the bishop of Rome... In fact, however, the church of Rome owed its eminence not so much to theoretical claims, which few were willing to concede, as to its position in the Roman Empire. The obvious center of the Christian faith in the early days was Jerusalem, where James, the brother of Christ, was active; but James' martyrdom in AD 62 and the destruction of Jerusalem in AD 70 opened the way for Rome.' [5]

As the church developed documents were enlisted to certify the historicity of Papal powers. In the fourth century one such document, the Pseudo-Clementine epistle of Clement to James, was supposedly composed and purported falsely to be the proof text for Roman claims. It shows how quickly the failure of the Roman community to possess a proof text supporting its claims was dealt with. This document was quoted in almost every Papal communication in the Middle Ages and was used repeatedly as the justification for Papal power.[6]

While the Catholic Church was developing its hegemony at Rome, another force was becoming prominent, anti-Semitism. It was promoted by the false testimony in the Gospels, especially John, and by the rabid, anti-Semitic tracts of bitter 'Church Fathers'. The good St. Ignatius, for one, was particularly adept at composing unwarranted and quarrelsome literature.[7] It is no wonder that racists everywhere have quoted the scriptures and saints as supporting their hate. Hitler, Rockwell, and Klan and the nineteenth century aristocrats of the Old South have certified their pronouncements with 'Bible and Church'.

The Church was not altogether bankrupt however. Learning was preserved in the monasteries. Historians like Eusebius attempted to preserve 'Church History'. Certain Popes, too, acted responsibly by sponsoring legislation aiding those Christians in adversity.

Protestantism, as Catholicism had hundreds of years before, developed unintentionally. What the Protestant Reformers did not understand was that the basic doctrines of the Church which they thought could be interpreted from the New Testament and related literature were laden with many of the same pagan doctrines of Catholicism. What most of them failed to grasp was that the Christian Church had not gone astray in the third or fourth centuries. Contamination of doctrine had started in the first century when the early movement became associated with the pagan world. To a rather remarkable degree the Reformers were only reverting to the less paganized and historically earlier interpretation of the faith. No attempt was made to go back to the earliest period because it was firmly believed that the Gospels and the Acts contained accurate information about Jesus and his followers. Further investigation of embryonic Christianity did not take place until the period of Enlightenment.

But Protestantism was a step in the right direction, since freedom on interpretation and the playing down of rigid positions on matters of doctrine fostered the heightened worth of the individual and the idea that mans' conscience should supersede the dogmatisms of Catholicism. The obvious advantage of the Protestant view is that mankind can be more responsible to fresh ideas and new historical discoveries. Catholicism is rigid and unable to meet the modern challenge as a marked decline in religious vocations, service attendance and the disintegration of educational institutions has sadly demonstrated.

In recent times many Catholics and Protestants have become more sophisticated in matters relating to Christianity and have tended to disregard much of what has been hammered into them save the social and moral aspects. This has resulted because of the unprecedented broad reach of mass communications. Twentieth century man more than ever before has been exposed to contrary information resulting from increased social and scientific research. Books, radio and television have turned out to be enemies of the frauds that the Church puts forth. No longer can a prudish old bachelor in Rome demand strict obedience on matters such as birth control, divorce, and weekly service attendance. Religious authorities everywhere are experiencing the revelation that they no longer can sell many of their congregation a bill of goods. Man to an ever increasing extent is asking 'Why' before answering 'Yes'. The greatest problem facing Churchman today is to somehow endow Jesus with a believably human personality who can relate to 21st century mankind, especially to the youth.

Study Aids

1. The best discussion of the differences between Hebrew and Christian Messiahs is by J. Klausner, Messianic Idea in Israel.

2. The dispute over Cambodia is a good example.

3. Murdoch H.B., The Development of the Papacy, where the subject is dealt with in some detail.

4. Catholics often quote Papias, 'Peter and Paul founded the church of Rome'. This statement is historically worthless, since Paul stated in Acts that he did not found the church at Rome.

5. Barraclough G., The Medieval Papacy, an excellent companion to Dr. Murdock's book mentioned in #3. See Ch. One.

6. Ullman W., Principles of (Papa) Government and Politics in the Middle Ages. It is the consensus of expert opinion today that the Clementine literature is bogus. Experts point out that the document listed in the chapter was worked over by a Christian scholar named Rufinus whose attitude was best described as willing to add on or interpolate information into pre-existing literature. There are words in the document that did not exist for 4-6 centuries after it was supposedly written. A scholar named Lorenzo Vala pointed out this to the Papacy in the Middle Ages and was silenced.

7. Ignat, Magnesians and Philadelphians.

Some New Testament Study Aids

Standard

The works listed below, do not represent the sum total of the sources used in the preparation of this book. Rather, it was my intention that the reader be introduced to the sources that New Testament scholars consider basic.

Apocalypse of Baruch, translated by Charles, Black (London, 1896).

Assumption of Moses, translated by Charles, Black (London 1897). Also The Testament of.

Bacon, Benjamin, Studies in Matthew, Constable (London 1930).

Brandon, Samuel, The Fall of Jerusalem and the Christian Church, S.P.C.K. (London 1956).

Burkitt, F.C., The Gospel History and its Transmission, T. and T. Clark (Edinburgh 1926).

Conybeare, F.C., The Origins of Christianity, University Books, 1958 (1909).

Eisler, Robert, Enigma of the Fourth Gospel, Methuen (London 1938).

Enoch, Book of, translated by Charles, Clarendon (Oxford 1893).

Eusebius, Ecclesiastical History, translated by Cruse, Bell (London 1894).

Frazer, James, The Golden Bough, MacMillan (London 1914).

Herford, R.T., Christianity in the Talmud and Midrash, Norgate (London 1903).

Heer, F., God's First Love, Weybright and Talley (New York 1967).

Heer, F., The Medieval World, Praeger Publishers, N.Y.

Ignatius, Epistles, translated by Lake, Heinemann (London)

Josephus, Flavius, Works, Heinemann (London).

Klausner, J., From Jesus to Paul, Allen, (London 1943).

Mishnah, The, translated by Danby, Oxford (London 1933).

Schoeps, H.J., Theologie und Geschichte des Judenchristentum (1952).

Schonfield, H.J., The Authentic New Testament, Dobson Books (1956).

Schweitzer, Albert, The Quest of the Historical Jesus, Black (Lond 1930).

Suetonius, The Lives of the Twelve Caesars, translated by Thomson, Bell (London 1911).

Tacitus, The Annals and History, translated by Church and Brodribb (London).

Talmud, (Jerusalem and Babylonian), standard editions.

Williams, Lukyn, The Hebrew-Christian Messiah, from the Warburton Lectures 1911-5.

Windisch, H. Der Untergang Jerusalems (Anno 70) im Urtheil der Christen und Juden,

Article in Theologisch Tijdschrift, Leiden, 1914

Der zweite Korinthbrief, Gottingen, 1924

Die katholischen Briefe, Tubingen, 1930

Der Hebraerbrief, Tubingen, 1931

Der messianische Krieg und das Urchsristentum, Tubingen, 1909.